Joe Stahlkuppe

Basset Hounds

Everything about Purchase, Care, Nutrition,
Breeding, Behavior, and Training

With 46 Color Photographs

Illustrations by Michele Earle-Bridges

BARRON'S

About the Author

Joe Stahlkuppe, a lifelong dog fancier and breeder, writes dog columns for several pet and general interest publications. A former U.S. Army journalist in Vietnam and teacher, he is also the author of Barron's *Irish Setters: A Complete Pet Owner's Manual, Great Danes: A Complete Pet Owner's Manual, American Pit Bull and Staffordshire Terriers: A Complete Pet Owner's Manual*, and *Poodles: A Complete Pet Owner's Manual*. Mr. Stahlkuppe lives with his wife, Cathie, on a small farm in Alabama and looks forward to teaching his granddaughter Ann Catherine about dogs.

Photo Credits

Barbara Augello: front cover, pages 32 top, 33 top, 37, 61 top; Bob Schwartz: inside front cover, inside back cover, back cover, pages 9 bottom, 13 top and bottom, 16, 17 top and bottom, 24, 25 top right, 32 bottom, 40, 41, 48, 60, 69, 77, 80, 81; Joan Balzarini: page 8; Toni Tucker: pages 4, 9 top, 12 top and bottom, 49, 56; Nance Photography: pages 25 top left and bottom, 28, 33 bottom, 45, 61 bottom, 68 bottom, 76; Jean Wentworth: pages 29, 68 top, 84, 85; Paulette Braun: page 57.

All inquiries should be addressed to:
Barron's Educational Series, Inc.
250 Wireless Boulevard
Hauppauge, NY 11788

International Standard Book No. 0-8120-9737-8

Library of Congress Catalog Card No. 96-47677

Library of Congress Cataloging-in-Publication Data
Stahlkuppe, Joe.
    Basset hounds : everything about purchase, care, nutrition, breeding behavior, and training / Joe Stahlkuppe ; illustrations by Michele Earle-Bridges.
        p.   cm.—(A complete pet owner's manual)
    Includes bibliographical references (p. 86) and index.
        ISBN 0-8120-9737-8
        1. Basset hound. I. Title. III. Series.
SF429.B2S73   1997
636.753'6—DC21   96-47677
                                                   CIP

Printed in China

19 18 17 16 15 14 13 12 11 10

Important Note

This pet owner's guide tells the reader how to buy and care for a basset hound. The author and the publisher consider it important to point out that the advice given in the book is meant primarily for normally developed puppies from a good breeder—that is, dogs of excellent physical health and good character.

Anyone who adopts a fully grown dog should be aware that the animal has already formed its basic impressions of human beings. The new owner should watch the animal carefully, including its behavior toward humans, and should meet the previous owner. If the dog comes from a shelter, it may be possible to get some information on the dog's background and peculiarities there. There are dogs that, as a result of bad experiences with humans, behave in an unnatural manner or may even bite. Only people that have experience with dogs should take in such animals.

Caution is further advised in the association of children with dogs, in meeting with other dogs, and in exercising the dog without a leash.

Even well-behaved and carefully supervised dogs sometimes do damage to someone else's property or cause accidents. It is therefore in the owner's interest to be adequately insured against such eventualities, and we strongly urge all dog owners to purchase a liability policy that covers their dog.

Contents

Even single bassets, like this handsome tricolor, are able to provide hours of happy hunting for an individual. Because bassets are such gregarious pack animals, it is usually more fun to go with more than one dog.

Preface

The basset hound is like a solid old friend—not very surprising but very dependable. This analogy is based on the hope that you have sought out the best basset possible, avoiding the "breed for greed" mass producers that can (and often do) cause great harm to any popular breed.

Bassets are among the most lovable—and loving—of all breeds. They aren't the most demonstrative of all breeds, but their sweet natures make up for any lack of extroverted, terrierlike displays of adoration and affection that may be missing in their makeup.

A good pet, a steady hunter, a reliable playmate for supervised children, the basset can handle all these jobs and still have time for a nap! Realizing that this is the most laid-back of dogs will help you in your choosing or skipping over the basset hound for another type of dog. If you do find that you like the slow, staid, and solid, you'll love the basset hound.

This book is respectfully dedicated to the memory of Russ and Judy Kohser of Pennsylvania. No two people on earth ever loved dogs, dog events, dog people, and each other more than did Russ and Judy.

I would like to recognize Clyde and Marguerite Thompson, two great basset people. I also want to thank an old friend, and true dog lover, Sandra McLeroy.

I would like to thank: Amanda Pisani who is the consummate dog book editor, Dr. Matthew Vriends, the world-famous author of nearly a hundred books on birds and animals, and Don Reis, Barron's Senior Editor and distinguished man of publishing. I especially want to acknowledge the contributions made to this book and my life by my wife Cathie, my son Shawn, and his wife Lisa. I also am living for the day when I can help my new granddaughter, Ann Catherine, choose a puppy of her own, perhaps even a basset puppy of her own.

Understanding Basset Hounds

The basset hound is one of the most recognizable dog breeds in the world. From a short-legged French hunting hound, the basset has become a sad-faced Renaissance dog. Transformed by television into a star, a corporate logo, and a regular media darling, this calm, long-bodied hound has millions of fans who know the breed only by its appearance.

Originally bred to be a solid, slow-moving pack dog, the basset is much more than "just another pretty face." The breed continues to win in the dog show ring and some bassets are quite able obedience trial dogs. An increasing number of basset hounds are returning to the field as rabbit

The appealing basset comes from a long history of hunting hounds for several types of game.

hounds or in the growing sport of basset field trialing.

Media star, best-in-show winner, magazine coverdog, the basset has come a long way from being a low-slung French rabbit dog. A master of subtle, sleepy charm, the basset has taken relaxation to new heights. Calm and unperturbable, the basset has taken its success in low, slow stride and still maintains a well-deserved reputation as an excellent family pet.

Origin and History

Over the centuries, the French developed many types of hunting dogs, especially hunting hounds. There may have been as many as a dozen varieties of these hounds that had very short legs, identified as *bas* or "low" hounds. Bred to work thick cover and heavy woods, these low-set hounds did not need the blazing speed of a greyhound, the size and fighting ability of the wolfhound, the agility of the foxhound, or even the merry quickness of the beagle. The basset hound depended on excellent scenting abilities, dogged perseverance, and endurance.

At a time when most hunters used primitive weapons such as spears, nets, and clubs, the slowness of the basset was a definite asset. Hunters could easily keep pace with bassets, depending on the sensitive nose of the short hounds to pick up and stay with scents other, speedier hounds would run right by.

Bloodhounds and Bassets

The sense of smell of the basset hound rivals that of its near kin and taller cousin, the bloodhound. The basset, except for its very short legs, is closer in type and personality to the bloodhound than it is to most of the other scent hound breeds. Both share many of the same abilities and some of the same problems.

Both the bloodhound and the basset hound are thought to be descendants of the legendary Saint Hubert hounds. Saint Hubert, a churchman who became the patron saint of hunting, was supposedly a widely regarded hunter and hunting dog fancier. During the sixth century he developed packs of hounds that were held in high esteem. After Hubert's death, the monks of his abbey continued to breed these hounds and often presented them to royalty.

Other Origins

Other origins for the basset hound include the probability of a genetic mutation for short legs that was found useful and that firmly established itself. Some authorities linked the basset hound and the dachshund in a plausible scenario where the two short-legged hunting breeds stemmed from common, low-slung forebears but took on different hunting roles, markedly different personalities, and a different appearance other than sharing a low height.

The exact ancient origins of the basset will probably remain unknown, but the more modern history of the breed involves several dedicated French dog breeders, many equally dedicated British supporters, and some American enthusiasts. This multinational approach ultimately brought this sad-faced, plodding hunting hound to a position of popularity throughout the world.

In France, the Comte le Couteulx de Canteleu, M. Louis Lane, M. Masson,

The basset hound and the bloodhound are descendants of the legendary Saint Hubert hounds, named for the patron saint of hunting. Other than leg length, the basset and the bloodhound share many of the same characteristics.

the Marquis de Tournon, M. Leon Verrier, and others were pivotal contributors to the development, standardization, and improvement of the basset hound. Starting with the divergent gene pool of short French hunting dogs, these key breeders each had somewhat different ideas about what they wanted in basset hounds, but each worked diligently to produce basset hounds of overall quality. Finally, a blending of these different strains (or families) of hounds gave an equally dedicated cadre of English breeders the foundation for what would become the modern basset hound.

In the late nineteenth century and early twentieth century, significant English fans of the basset hound were Lords Galway and Onslow, the Prince and Princess of Wales, and Queen Alexandra. Perhaps the most important English breeder was Sir Everett Millais. Sir Everett studied the best of the French hounds, conducted a myriad of breeding and cross-breeding experiments, imported the best of

The basset is confident, a little stubborn, and among the most photogenic of dogs.

French bassets, and thoroughly championed the breed. It was through his efforts that the basset hound attracted the attention of English dog breeding society, and subsequently, American dog breeders.

Arriving in the United States

Short-legged French hounds of the *bas* sort had been brought to North America for more than 100 years before 1885 when the first basset hound was registered with the American Kennel Club. Sources suggest that George Washington received some of these short hounds, referred to by some sources as "bench-legged beagles," from the Marquis de Lafayette. Many other dog breeders and sporting dog enthusiasts brought earlier versions of the sturdy basset to the United States. There were many Americans who brought dogs directly from France; others favored British importations. Some American dog fanciers turned to both sources for the best available bassets. One of the most significant of these American

basset fans was Gerald Livingston, who became informally known as the "father of the American basset hound." Livingston did much to bring the French hound, which was improved by the British, to the attention and then to the kennels of the American dog-owning public. His influence is still felt in the breed today as is the influence of great dogs that he produced.

In 1935 the Basset Hound Club of America was founded and in 1937 this organization was accepted as the official breed club by the American Kennel Club. This recognition was all the basset hound needed to begin its ascent up the ranks of popular breeds.

Personality

The basset hound is a paradox when it comes to personality. In many ways these short hounds have such sad-eyed charm that it is hard to imagine that they can also be stubborn and independent. Bassets can be the best of pets, but they need good, consistent training and discipline. People who want to add a basset to their family should become knowledgeable about the breed in order to provide the best kind of home for this breed, which is usually calm, except when on a hot scent.

As with many breeds that have achieved a high degree of public acceptance, recognition, and popularity, the basset hound is sometimes perceived as more plaything than pet. Bassets and potential basset owners deserve a more realistic and humane fate. Bassets are short but not small dogs. They are breathing, living creatures, not plush stuffed animals to be brought out to elicit oohs and ahhs from friends and neighbors.

Bassets are adorable as puppies and appealing as adults. They are among the most photogenic of all dogs during all stages of their lives. They are, however, still dogs, and will need the things most dogs need. They will want the things most dogs want. They will make the mistakes that most dogs do. Humans who want a really good dog as a pet can often find just what they want in the basset, but people who want some canine conversation piece should save themselves, and an innocent dog, the trouble.

The basset hound can be a fine family pet. It can be good in the field, in the show ring, and in obedience work—*if* it wants to be! The task for any basset owner is to encourage, develop, and help the basset in doing the right things! Unfortunately, some owners fall for that hangdog expression, that long and low body, and the stubby legs, and see the basset hound as something too cute to control, or too appealing to discipline. This is an error of large proportions and can hurt an otherwise excellent dog.

Basset hounds are still very capable of living up to their hunting hound heritage. This stately red and white dog seems quite comfortable in a rural setting.

Companion and Family Pet

The basset hound can be a great companion animal. Usually sweet and loving, the basset seems to fit in very well with its human owners. Slow and deliberate most of the time, the basset hound is not a dog for the hyperactive owner. It goes along best at its own pace and in activities that fit its demeanor and physical stature. A thoughtful individual or family that is considering a basset should always keep this in mind. The person who wants to challenge for the national championship in Frisbee catching should pick another breed!

Bassets are loving companions for humans of all ages. Perhaps a part of their pack hound heritage, the basset can develop a special, individualized bond with each person in a family. They are sturdy enough for supervised play with children. They are certainly calm enough to spend a quiet day at home, and can more than hold their own as hunting and tracking dogs. In addition, bassets from show dog backgrounds

can be excellent in the show ring. While maybe not the dog for everyone, the basset hound can fill the need for many people seeking an affectionate, attractive, super calm family pet.

Originally bred to be amiable in large packs, the basset hound has kept its even temper, as these two bassets clearly demonstrate.

Ranking only slightly lower than the bloodhound in scenting ability, the basset has made its way from being a hunter to being a housepet.

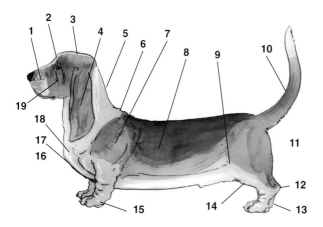

The anatomy of the basset hound:
1. muzzle, 2. stop, 3. skull, 4. ear,
5. neckline, 6. withers, 7. shoulder,
8. rib cage, 9. loin, 10. tail, 11. hindquarters,
12. hock, 13. rear pastern, 14. stifle,
15. front pastern, 16. forequarters,
17. brisket, 18. chest, 19. cheek.

Family Responsibility

Each family member needs to take special care of this special pet. The basset can be injured if a small child perceives the dog as a long, short pony and tries to ride it—basset backs are not designed for such stress. If older children leave doors or gates open, a nose-following basset can trail its way away from home. Its poor sense of direction can then prevent the dog from back-tracking and returning. Often so intent on following a delicious-smelling scent, a loose basset can follow a track right into a roadway and tragedy.

Young bassets, with their abnormally long bodies and heavily built fronts and chests need to be kept off the couch, off the bed, even off low walls. This low-to-the-ground canine is not meant for jumping and hurdling. Many broken bones, strains, and other preventable injuries can be avoided by keeping the basset out of harm's way.

Both the eyes and ears of the basset are droopy and right at a level where some potentially dangerous injury-maker can hurt them. A basset's family must take responsibility for this slow, lovable pet that may not recognize the things that can hurt it.

Bassets like to eat, sometimes don't get enough exercise, and are thus subject to obesity that can shorten their lives and cause painful physical problems. They can be subject, as are other deep-chested dogs, to gastric tortion (or bloat) (see page 72). Their deeply wrinkled facial skin requires some special care and cleaning. Water is inviting, but swimming is difficult for the basset who could tumble into the family pool and drown.

One dog show judge referred to the calm demeanor of the basset as "rather like the first stages of a coma, slow motion, or sleepwalking." Bassets do like their beauty rest. Low activity levels make them the opposite of some terriers and other breeds that are almost in perpetual motion. Bassets do run and have a good time, but they do it in their own way, which can sometimes seem like the basset is being stubborn. A patient, but persistent dog owner can win out because the basset is also usually not demanding or aggressive.

The basset can take a little longer to become housebroken than other breeds. (See Housebreaking, page 40) Patience and persistence are also needed here. This excellent family pet needs just a little more encouragement and support than some other breeds to understand when and where it · needs to go to relieve itself.

Bassets, even with their shortcomings, can be among the gentlest, most loving of pets. Their calm dispositions make them an excellent pet for the right owner. When a thoroughly prepared dog owner finds the right basset, and gives it the right care, the result can be one of the best of dog-human companion relationships.

In the Show Ring

The basset hound may seem homely to some people, but this short hound has many admirers among the dog show crowd. While maintaining its capacity to be a good pet, and an able sporting dog, the basset has also firmly established itself in the highly competitive world of conformation dog shows. This short but charismatic hound is always a favorite with the crowds that visit dog shows.

Veteran dog breeders and handlers tell of an interesting metamorphosis that seems to come over many a sleepy-appearing basset when it is time to enter exhibition competition. A show-quality basset, which may have slept for hours in apparently relaxed boredom before time to enter the show ring, will often become showy (in a basset sort of way), projecting a win-

Bassets can pick up a delicious scent and in a very determined manner follow it away from home and into the way of trouble, possibly injury or death!

some and winning image to the dog show judge and to all other onlookers. Other bassets have to be awakened to go to the show ring and seem more concerned in getting the judging over so they can finish their naps.

Quality exhibition bassets come from quality exhibition stock. They are usually groomed, trained, and prepared for a show career if they are to achieve greatness in the show ring. Aided by the variety of attractive basset hound colors and markings, these dogs win their share of top awards.

Obedience Trial Work

While the hound group as a rule is overshadowed in obedience trials by other breed classifications, there are some hounds represented there. The basset is no exception. Some bassets are more difficult to train than others, but the breed can certainly be successful in obedience work.

Experienced dog trainers and novices alike have campaigned their low-slung students to highly prized titles. Not as numerous in numbers in these activities (few hound breeds

Bassets sometime have real difficulty swimming. Reasonable care should always be taken when bassets are near lakes, ponds, or swimming pools.

are), bassets have won several titles and do very well in aspects of obedience that emphasize trailing, tracking, and scenting abilities.

The public may think of the basset as sort of a sad clown of a dog, but this show dog gives ample evidence of what the basset hound can do in a show ring situation.

Obedience trial dogs are often one-person dogs; they need to please one human over all others. This bond is helpful in training, but it can lead to an exclusivity that keeps some obedience dogs from interacting as successfully with strangers and other family members. None of this is a problem for bassets; they love everybody. Their noses also serve as distraction-providers. A pleasing scent can take some bassets' minds right off the task at hand.

Perils of Popularity

Bassets suffer from popularity as do many other breeds. Informed advocates of most breeds dread, rather than embrace, great popularity for their favorite varieties. They have learned that when a breed becomes popular, its overall quality may decline.

The photogenic basset has become internationally well known. A popular television show from the 1950s, "The People's Choice," starring former child star Jackie Cooper, featured Cleo, a red-and-white female basset. Cleo's character was also "heard" in a voice-over and often had the show's best lines. Cleo became an instant success and helped increase basset popularity.

Another early TV basset was Pokey who shared the small screen with no less a canine legend than Lassie, him/herself, and belonged to Lassie's young owner's best friend. Still another basset to achieve widespread recognition was the basset logo for a popular brand of leisure shoes. Perhaps chosen as an image for this product to accent relaxation, the basset has served as the major marketing tool for these shoes for decades.

Popularity for a dog breed always has its price. When a breed is relatively unknown to the general public, it is usually bred by experienced, knowledgeable fans who strive for high quality. When a breed achieves wide popularity, inexperienced people allow dogs of lesser quality to reproduce because popularity always guarantees a quick-sale market for the resulting puppies. That some of these puppies may have behavioral or physical defects, or genetically transmitted problems, doesn't seem to occur to, or matter to, some of these people.

Ultimately, a popular breed will suffer as more and more poor-quality specimens are produced. Bad behavior or health problems fueled by poor breeding practices become part of the public's conception of a particular popular breed, whether it is true or not. Many dog people say that the greater the popularity of the breed, the more careful should be the search for a dog or puppy of that breed.

The Basset Personality Summary

There are a number of canine personality indicators that can give a reasonably accurate overview of bassets as a breed:

Overall activity level: Quite low.

Barking: Neither silent, nor excessively noisy. This also makes the basset less effective in barking at intruders.

Territoriality: As would be natural for a pack hound breed, not very concerned about "turf" rights. Aggressive behavior by a basset toward other dogs is still well below such behavior, on average, of all dog breeds but male bassets do show such aggressiveness more than do females.

Human interaction: Not likely to bite small children, nor likely to try to gain control over the humans in the household. Though very sweet and loving dogs, bassets don't need the constant pats of reassurance from their owners that some breeds require.

Trainability: Not top obedience scholars although some bassets do well enough in obedience training to

Sweet-natured with an appealing appearance, the basset hound has become extremely popular.

Will the real basset hound please stand up? The basset is a real dog, not some animated toy. A real dog deserves real care from real people.

While the basset may be relaxed at home, he can show his regal side and charisma when called upon to do so.

win titles. Bassets, especially males, can be difficult to housebreak.

Behavior: Enjoy their own level of participation in play. Don't expect the average basset to frisk and frolic in the same way one would expect from the more active terrier breeds. Bassets also are not as likely to engage in destructive behaviors as much as many breeds.

American Kennel Club Standard for the Basset Hound

General Appearance—The Basset Hound possesses in marked degree those characteristics which equip it admirably to follow a trail over and through difficult terrain. It is a short-legged dog, heavier in bone, size considered, than any other breed of dog, and while its movement is deliberate, it is in no sense clumsy. In temperament it is mild, never sharp or timid. It is capable of great endurance in the field and is extreme in its devotion.

Head—The head is large and well proportioned. Its length from occiput to

muzzle is greater than the width at the brow. In over-all appearance the head is of medium width. The **skull** is well domed, showing a pronounced occipital protuberance. A broad flat skull is a fault. The length from nose to stop is approximately the length from stop to occiput. The sides are flat and free from cheek bumps. Viewed in profile the top lines of the muzzle and skull are straight and lie in parallel planes, with a moderately defined stop. The skin over the whole of the head is loose, falling in distinct wrinkles over the brow when the head is lowered. A dry head and tight skin are faults. The **muzzle** is deep, heavy, and free from snipiness. The **nose** is darkly pigmented, preferably black, with large wide-open nostrils. A deep liver-colored nose conforming to the coloring of the head is permissible but not desirable. The **teeth** are large, sound, and regular, meeting in either a scissors or an even bite. A bite either overshot or undershot is a serious fault. The **lips** are darkly pigmented and are pendulous, falling squarely in front and, toward the back, in loose hanging flews. The **dewlap** is very pronounced. The **neck** is powerful, of good length, and well arched. The **eyes** are soft, sad, and slightly sunken, showing a prominent haw, and in color are brown, dark brown preferred. A somewhat lighter-colored eye conforming to the general coloring of the dog is acceptable but not desirable. Very light or protruding eyes are faults. The **ears** are extremely long, low set, and when drawn forward, fold well over the end of the nose. They are velvety in texture, hanging in loose folds with the ends curling slightly inward. They are set far back on the head at the base of the skull and, in repose, appear to be set on the neck. A high set or flat ear is a serious fault.

Forequarters—The **chest** is deep and full with prominent sternum showing clearly in front of the legs. The

shoulders and elbows are set close against the sides of the chest. The distance from the deepest point of the chest to the ground, while it must be adequate to allow free movement when working in the field, is not to be more than one-third the total height at the withers of an adult basset. The shoulders are well laid back and powerful. Steepness in shoulder, fiddle fronts, and elbows that are out, are serious faults. The **forelegs** are short, powerful, heavy in bone, with wrinkled skin. Knuckling over of the front legs is a disqualification. The **paw** is massive, very heavy with tough heavy pads, well rounded and with both feet inclined equally a trifle outward, balancing the width of the shoulders. Feet down at the pastern are a serious fault. The **toes** are neither pinched together nor splayed, with the weight of the forepart of the body borne evenly on each. The dewclaws may be removed.

Body—The rib structure is long, smooth, and extends well back. The ribs are well sprung, allowing adequate room for heart and lungs. Flatsidedness and flanged ribs are faults. The topline is straight, level, and free from any tendency to sag or roach, which are faults.

Hindquarters—The hindquarters are very full and well rounded, and are approximately equal to the shoulders in width. They must not appear slack or light in relation to the over-all depth of the body. The dog stands firmly on its hind legs showing a well-let-down stifle with no tendency toward a crouching stance. Viewed from behind, the hind legs are parallel, with the hocks turning neither in nor out. Cowhocks or bowed legs are serious faults. The hind feet

point straight ahead. Steep, poorly angulated hindquarters are a serious fault. The dewclaws, if any, may be removed.

Tail—The tail is not to be docked, and is set in continuation of the spine with but slight curvature, and carried gaily in hound fashion. The hair on the underside of the tail is coarse.

Size—The height should not exceed 14 inches. Height over 15 inches at the highest point of the shoulder blades is a disqualification.

Gait—The Basset Hound moves in a smooth, powerful, and effortless manner. Being a scenting dog with short legs, it holds its nose low to the ground. Its gait is absolutely true with perfect coordination between the front and hind legs, and it moves in a straight line with hind feet following in line with the front feet, the hocks well bent with no stiffness of action. The front legs do not paddle, weave, or overlap, and the elbows must lie close to the body. Going away, the hind legs are parallel.

Coat—The coat is hard, smooth, and short, with sufficient density to be of use in all weather. The skin is loose and elastic. A distinctly long coat is a disqualification.

Color—Any recognized hound color is acceptable and the distribution of color and markings is of no importance.

DISQUALIFICATIONS
Height of more than 15 inches at the highest point of the shoulder blades.
Knuckled over front legs.
Distinctly long coat.

Living with a Basset Hound

Sharing your life with a basset hound is an enjoyable experience made even more so if you understand the uniqueness of the breed. Trying to mold the calm and docile basset into another type of dog will be a mistake—let the basset hound be just what it is and you will usually be very pleased with the result.

Not Tall, but Not Small

The basset hound is not a small dog; it is a large dog with short legs. Males can routinely weigh 50 pounds (22.7 kg) or more while standing only 14 inches (36 cm) high at the shoulder. The basset packs a lot of dog into a long, low-slung package. This fairly uncommon canine form brings with it some special considerations.

The basset hound lives life down where many potential indoor and outdoor dangers exist: sharp corners, briars, protruding wires, and so on. Many hazards are at basset-eye level or lower where they could damage the underside of the basset.

As House Pets

The basset is not built to be a lapdog. The average person might even have difficulty picking up an adult basset, and such handling, if done incorrectly, could injure this long-bodied dog. Young bassets should *NEVER* be allowed to go up or down stairs, as stairs can put great physical stress on their still developing front legs and chest.

Many basset experts suggest that basset hounds should be discouraged from getting on couches, easy chairs, and beds designed for humans; getting up on and down from furniture exposes bassets to many possible injuries. Training bassets to stay off furniture

Living with a basset can be a delightful experience for the owner that makes a real effort to understand the breed. This dog has a flair for posing, a trait many bassets seem to have.

This basset has its best guard dog face on. Bassets might bark at an intruder, but if the intruder had some food to share the basset might also leave with him.

Bassets are usually no threat to any other pets. This kitten seems to have the upper paw in its relationship with this large, mellow basset hound.

Bassets, like all other dogs, will do what they are allowed to do. Keeping these very relaxed pets off the family couch or the recliner will require consistent, and early, reinforcement that people have their places and bassets have theirs.

isn't as difficult as it is with other more active and affection-seeking breeds.

Bassets can do well living inside or outside. Owners need more patience to housebreak male bassets than they do for housebreaking females, but a persistent owner can handle this training task. The basset fits in well with most families. Families with swimming pools need to be aware that some bassets don't swim well and can become disoriented about where the shallow end of the pool is. Just as you would with small children, safeguard bassets by limiting access to pools.

Bassets and Children

Bassets make great pets for children. Adult basset hounds are large enough for the play of even very enthusiastic children. Bassets are low on the list of dog breeds that often bite children, and low regarding domination and aggressiveness. Bassets aren't

going to be as active as some terrier breeds, but neither will they be constantly jumping up on small children and knocking them down.

While a great pet for children, care must be taken to keep children from jumping on the back of a basset hound or attempting to ride it. Because the skeletal structure of basset hounds is different from most other breeds, they must be protected from injuries that could be serious.

Children should always realize and remember that basset hounds were and are trailing hounds—they go where their noses lead them. If a basset is allowed to roam loose in a neighborhood or on a farm, it could follow an interesting scent away from its home. At the very least, the basset could get lost. At worst, it could become injured or killed while single-mindedly following a scent. All doors and gates must *ALWAYS* be kept closed and children need to know this will protect their basset pet.

Bassets and Other Pets

Bassets are very good with other animals. They easily learn to share a household with cats and with other animals. Being bred to work cooperatively with other hounds in a pack, bassets have an innate lack of aggressiveness.

Some kennels that raise bassets have proven the good nature of the breed. It is not uncommon for several stud dogs to be kept together in the same run and sharing the same dog-house. This is also true of brood bitches. Puppies, even those of differing ages, can often be housed together after they have been weaned and are awaiting new homes. There are few other breeds that could safely be housed in this manner.

Bassets' sweet nature and easygoing ways make them good house pets in homes where there are other animals.

Bassets as Guard Dogs

Bassets generally love everybody. They aren't much use as guard dogs and don't even bark in a watchdog manner very often. Owners of bassets should depend on something other than their sorrowful-looking hounds to protect home and property.

Bassets are even easy dogs to steal; they will follow friendly strangers if allowed to do so. Bloodhounds and bassets are first cousins and a blood-hound story also fits for basset hounds: A bloodhound was bred and trained to track fleeing prisoners or criminals. The hound's handler released the dog from its harness and the bloodhound raced well ahead and caught up with the fugitive, whereupon the fugitive and the dog went on together. The bloodhound was sold in the next town, giving the prisoner enough money to make good his escape!

Bassets and children can make wonderful companions. Very young children should always be supervised by adults. No child should be allowed to attempt to ride on the basset hound's back!

19

Caring for Basset Hounds

Bassets don't want much: a place to sleep, food, water, and an occasional pat or a friendly word. A few more things are required to give bassets adequate care. As trailing hounds they need to be confined in some manner all the time to keep them from following a trail away from home and family and possibly into harm's way. This confinement can be inside the house, in a fenced backyard or kennel run, on a leash when out on walks, or through proper training.

Housing—Inside

The best way to keep bassets, or any other dogs, in your home is to

A well-built doghouse will provide protection from drafts, from rain or snow, and from the effects of too much sunshine.

make use of a cage, crate, or carrier (see The Cage/Crate/Carrier, page 39). Dogs are naturally denning creatures. If left to their own devices, they will find some place in your home to serve as their own, personal den—under a table in an out-of-the-way place, in a closet, or even behind a piece of furniture. By using a crate or carrier, you can establish where the dog's den will be.

Cages, crates, and carriers have revolutionized the way that house dogs can be made more comfortable and also are invaluable in housebreaking. Not only does a dog instinctively need a place of its own, they also don't like to mess up these places by defecating or urinating there. Making use of these two instincts can help your basset become a much better house pet. Even if your dog goes outside to a doghouse and fenced yard, a cage/crate/carrier for inside your home is one of the best investments you can make.

Housing—Outside

Although most basset fans believe their favorite breed should be housebroken and live in the house with its owners, your basset can function well both inside and outside the home. A fenced yard with a snug doghouse can be a good place for your basset to stay when it is not with you.

If a fenced yard is not possible, a fenced kennel run with a doghouse is also an option. Without some fenced outside area, your basset must either stay inside or go outside only when you are along. Because of its propensity for roaming away from home following a trail, no basset can simply be put outside in complete safety.

The doghouse should be placed out of direct sunlight. There are many designs, but the best house will have a way for the dog to get out of direct drafts (see the doghouse drawing on page 20.) In cold climates your basset should probably be inside with you unless its own house is thoroughly insulated and adequately ventilated. Warm areas of the country require that the doghouse have more ventilation.

Inside or out, bassets will need protection from pests like fleas and ticks (see pages 70 and 71). They will also require as much clean and fresh water as they want. If bassets are fed outside, they should be fed on a regular schedule and any uneaten food taken away.

Every member of the household should make certain that gates and doors are always closed, after going out or coming in, to protect the family basset from wandering away. Fenced yards are an absolute must for basset hounds!

Exercising Your Basset

Bassets have only moderate exercise needs. Care should be taken with puppies and very young adults to not overdo exercise in order to avoid causing damage to still developing bones and muscles. One of the best forms of exercise for your basset is to go for walks with the dog during relief breaks. Both dog and owner can benefit from such regular strolling, with steps to match the basset's.

If your basset spends much time in a fenced backyard, it will usually get enough exercise, but additional activities require exercise to keep a basset in shape. A basset that hunts, a breeding animal, a show dog, or an obedience performer will need to be in good condition for these extra roles.

Moderate exercise is always needed as a way to battle that great canine killer, obesity. With a sensible diet, exercise can help bassets keep off those extra pounds that also can eventually cripple a long-bodied dog.

Special Basset Hound Care

Your basset is low to the ground and problems can sometimes result on the dog's undercarriage. Females can have scratches or abrasions on their teats; males can have similar injuries on the sheath that protects their penis; therefore, regularly check the underside of your basset to be certain that all is well.

Bassets will need special feeding to avoid age-related problems in youngsters or obesity in older dogs (see Feeding Bassets at Different Ages, beginning on page 62). Poor feeding practices can also do harm to the skeletal development of your basset. Make nutrition for your dog a high-priority concern and learn how to avoid problems that start in the food bowl and could result in a shortened life for your pet.

Warning: Remember that as a scent hound your basset can trail itself away from home. Protect your pet from becoming another lost dog.

HOW-TO:
Grooming Your Basset

Along with regular use of a slicker brush and a regular bristled brush, a grooming mitt, sometimes called a "hound glove" can be used to groom the basset's short, but thick, coat.

Trimming Toenails

Because of their high ratio of weight to height, bassets put a lot of stress on their feet. More active dogs, running over stones or on concrete surfaces, may wear down their toenails, but bassets will need their owners' help to avoid foot problems resulting from overgrown toenails.

Toenail trimming should begin as soon as you get a basset puppy and should continue regularly at intervals of every ten days to two weeks for the entire life of the dog. Some dogs, especially those that have not had their nails trimmed from early puppyhood, may be skittish about having some person handling their feet. By starting early, gradually, gently, and regularly, bassets can learn that trimming is nothing to fear.

The basset hound, because of its weight and unique body, is susceptible to a number of foot problems. Some of these can be avoided by regular (every 10 days to two weeks) trimming of the dog's toenails.

The owner should not fear nail trimming either. You can trim your pet's nails yourself with a good pair of trimmers. There are two kinds of nail trimmers, the scissors type and the guillotine type. The scissors nail trimmers are similar to snips used to trim metal or branches. The guillotine nail trimmers require placing the nail through an opening and snipping it off with the blade that goes downward from the handle.

Your veterinarian can show you how to trim your basset's nails. Practice on round toothpicks until you cut off just the tip of the nail, avoiding the "quick" or center of the nail that contains a vein. This vein will bleed profusely if you cut the nail too short.

When you check your dog's nails always check the feet and toes for cuts, bruises, foreign materials like splinters, and other potential problems. Your basset will need to be given regular care for both grooming and health reasons.

Brushing

Thoroughly brush your basset hound with a grooming mitt or a brush with bristles. Shedding coats will require either a shedding rake or a slicker brush to get out as much dead hair as possible. Starting with its head, carefully but gently brush the dog repeatedly. Use a fine-toothed metal comb for sensitive areas and places where the brush or slicker cannot easily reach.

Bathing

As with their toenails, basset hounds should be bathed early in their lives to get them accustomed to this routine event. Breed experts point out that teaching a basset to submit to its bath when it weighs five pounds (2.3 kg) is better than waiting until the dog weighs 50 pounds (22.3 kg). Baths should only be given often enough to keep your basset clean—too many baths will dry a dog's skin and coat.

Bathtime for a basset should not be a long, drawn-out procedure. Using a very mild dog shampoo and warm water, wash the dog, paying special attention to thorough rinsing. Dry the dog carefully with thick towels or with an electric hair dryer, being careful not to have the dryer too hot or the basset can be burned in the process.

Eyes: The basset hound's eyes are large and soap will irritate them. Keep soap and soapy water out of its eyes and use a sterile petrolatum ophthalmic ointment as a precautionary step to protect them. After the bath use a regular over-the-counter eyewash and gently wipe the eyes with a soft cloth or a cotton ball to make certain that no bath residue remains.

Ears: Use a similar process with the basset hound's ears. Be certain to keep shampoo and soapy water out of them. Some breeders put cotton balls in the ear canals to be sure that no water gets in there. Because the basset's ears are so large and hang so low they get covered with dirt, bits of food, and other foreign material. Ears

The basset hound's long ears should be checked daily—it is helpful to have one person steady the dog's head while another person cleans or applies medication to the dog's ears.

should get special cleaning attention both at bathtimes and in between. Using cotton with a mild astringent, or wipes used for human babies, thoroughly clean the ears, but only up to the cotton balls (which should be removed after each bath) that you may have inserted into the ear canals.

Basset ears deserve a daily check to see that they are free from parasites, such as ear mites and ticks, and that they don't have small injuries or ear problems. Start checking and washing your basset's ears while it is still a puppy and the process will be not only healthful for the dog, but less of a struggle for you.

Tooth Care

An important part of grooming your basset involves keeping the dog's teeth and gums in good health. Inexperienced dog owners are advised to have any excessive tartar on their pet's teeth removed by a veterinarian, but, with some experience, you cannot only brush your basset's teeth yourself, but also do minor tartar removal with a tartar scraper.

Every time you check your basset's eyes and ears, take a moment to check its teeth. Look for tartar, but also for foreign objects such as bits of food or wood slivers. Dog biscuits and various types of chew toys can help reduce tartar buildup but can't be expected to remove all tartar or replace regular dental care.

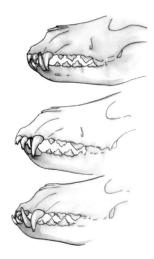

How a dog's teeth come together is called its bite; Top—scissors bite, Center—overbite, Bottom—underbite.

Anal Sacs

Regular grooming also includes checking your dog's two anal sacs, located on either side of the anus. If these are not emptied regularly, they can become impacted and possibly infected. Impaction often results in "scooting" behavior, where a dog drags its rear end along the floor. Use a cotton ball or a tissue to clear out the unpleasant smelling fluid from these sacs. Holding the dog's tail up and out of the way with one hand, carefully and gently squeeze each sac, which should cause an expelling of the anal sac contents. If you can't empty the sacs in this way, see your veterinarian for professional assistance.

Bassets have a special look that seems to say, "Feed Me!" Bassets are prone to become overweight. Even a charming fellow like this one needs help to prevent obesity, which can be crippling to basset hounds.

Bassets need only moderate exercise, but they need it regularly. Walking is good if done at a pace that is comfortable for the short-legged hound.

Bassets remain what they have been for hundreds of years—scent hounds. Unless they are securely kept inside a home, in a kennel run, or in a fenced backyard, the basset is prone to follow its nose away from home.

Traveling with a basset hound can be fun, but it can also be a chore. Even on short trips, like this one to the country, always make certain that your first concerns are the safety and comfort of the dog.

Traveling with Your Basset

Bassets may not be the easiest dogs with which to travel, but you can take trips with them. The safety and comfort of your basset hound should always be your first consideration. If the dog is very young or very old, or if some health problem is present, you may want to skip the trip yourself or leave your hound at home.

One key rule is that your basset should always travel in its crate or carrier; riding without restraint in a moving vehicle can be dangerous. Sharp curves, sudden stops, or even minor traffic accidents can cause a dog to become a canine missile flying around in the car at a surprisingly high speed. Do your basset a favor and keep it in a carrier.

Traveling by Air

Traveling by airplane is much safer for dogs than it was some years ago, but some canine fatalities still occur each year. Travel by air requires that your basset make use of an airline-approved carrier. If you don't use a carrier for your dog's den at home, you can probably rent one from your pet supply store or from the airline on which you plan to travel.

There are some good rules to observe when even considering traveling by air with your basset:

1. Call the airlines well before departure time to get a copy of their rules, procedures, and suggestions on how to make your basset's flight a safe and successful one.

2. Have your basset hound thoroughly examined by your veterinarian to make certain your pet is in good condition to make what could be a stressful trip. Your veterinarian can also provide the airline-required health certificate that your basset will need. If your veterinarian thinks your dog should stay home, follow this sound, professional advice.

3. Make your reservations, and those for your basset hound, well ahead of your estimated departure date. Get a direct flight to your destination to avoid having to change planes. Even if you have to drive to a hub airport to get a direct flight, it may keep you and your basset on the same plane.

4. If you are traveling to another country, be sure that your basset fits all entry requirements to go into and out of the country you are visiting.

5. Make certain that the carrier for your dog's flight, whether yours or a rental, is in good shape with all screws tightened and the door and latch in proper working order. You may also want to be certain that the necessary "conversion kit" for water is attached to the outside of the carrier.

6. Affix "Live Animal" stickers in easy-to-see locations on the carrier and have your name on a luggage tag along with your home phone number and a number where you can be reached at your destination.

7. Place a freshly laundered pad or blanket in the carrier to make it more comfortable for your basset hound.

8. Do not feed your pet for eight hours before departure. You can let the dog exercise and have water before the flight but don't put any food or water in the carrier other than in the external kit.

9. Unless you are certain that your destination has some of the same food your basset hound is used to eating, pack enough for the trip or send some ahead. Also be certain to pack any medications that your pet may need.

10. Your basset is important to you. Most airline employees are professional and humane, but impress upon them that you want to make certain that your basset hound arrives safely. Some dog owners take a photo of their dog with them. Others even take a picture of the dog in its carrier as it is being loaded on the plane.

Traveling by Automobile

Car travel with a basset hound is not as difficult as air travel, but there are some good suggestions to follow:

1. Remember to use a carrier, or a doggy safety harness whenever your basset is riding in a car.

2. On longer trips stop every hour or so to give your basset a breather, a drink of water, and a chance to relieve itself. Whenever you make these rest stops always keep your basset on a leash.

3. *Never leave your basset in a parked car, even with windows rolled down, during the day when temperatures are as high as 60°F (16°C).*

4. Check with auto clubs and with national motel-hotel chains to find places that allow pets to stay with their owners in their rooms. Don't try to sneak your basset into a motel or hotel; in many places this is against the law.

Boarding Your Basset

If you can't take your basset with you, you may be able to board your pet. Some boarding options are:

• Ask your veterinarian or pet supply store to recommend reputable pet sitters. These pet sitters should be licensed, bonded, and able to provide references from pet owners they have worked with. Always check out these references carefully before entrusting your dog and your home to a stranger.

• You may have a friend, neighbor, or family member who can care for your pet. Your basset hound could go for a visit or even stay at home and be cared for with this arrangement.

• Your veterinarian can probably put your basset up for a few days. This might also be a good time for a thorough checkup.

• There are some excellent boarding kennels in most areas. These kennels are accredited with the American Boarding Kennel Association (ABKA) (see Useful Addresses and Literature, page 86).

This little girl and this basset puppy will probably become best friends, if the child is carefully supervised by adults until she understands how to properly care for her canine pal.

Before You Buy a Basset Hound

Before you consider bringing a basset hound into your life, you need to give the matter a great deal of thought. Any pet will need your love and your attention, and a basset hound will need your special attention to keep it safe and healthy.

Not Just Another Pretty Face

Humans have produced more than 300 separate breeds of dogs worldwide. Some of these breeds are quite utilitarian in purpose, such as the greyhound and the basset. Both breeds also have gained many friends for their pet qualities, but their utilitarian aspects remain, and must be considered.

The basset is a charmingly sad-looking breed that wins people over by its appearance and sweet disposition. It isn't overly active, too demanding, or prone to moodiness. The basset is a hound. As a hound its primary instincts are to follow scents. Following scents takes precedence over most other aspects of basset life, other than sleeping and eating.

The basset and its bigger cousin, the bloodhound, have the best scenting abilities of all dogs. Both breeds descended from centuries-old hunting hound breeds. Both breeds are wrinkled and have long ears, characteristics that contribute to trailing by wafting the scent toward the hound's nose and, in the case of the wrinkling, retaining the scent to help keep the hound aware of it.

The appearance of the basset may be appealing. They may be among the most photogenic, and photographed, dogs. They may be used as logos and pitch-dogs for various products, but bassets are still hounds. Failing to consider that a pet basset, generations removed from hunting, is other than a hound is a mistake. Such a mistake can potentially bring harm to the gentle, homely-handsome basset.

Being a Consistent Dog Owner

All breeds of dogs need and deserve owners that will be consistent. Bassets may need this consistency even more than some other breeds. Because of the possibility of health problems brought on by poor feeding practices,

Owning a basset is much more than owning a cute pet. The basset hound will look to you for all of its needs, food, shelter, companionship, medical care, safety. Be sure you are up to the job.

the constant threat of a basset following an interesting smell away from home, the patience needed in some basset training, and the highly specialized physique of the basset, consistency in these areas is essential.

Bassets will eat many things but they will thrive only on a carefully balanced diet. Bassets can be happy inside or outside the home, but they must have a secure environment that keeps them at home. They weren't bred from centuries of successful house pets. Training for a basset is a little more involved and requires a little more attention than it does with some breeds. The long spine and almost gnarled front legs of the breed demand special arrangements to keep them from being injured in doing even everyday things that other breeds do.

To be a good and consistent basset owner, you will need to do the same things, the same way, each time. In feeding, kenneling, training, and safeguarding, the basset will do best if its owner is aware of these special needs and consistent in filling them.

Searching for the Right Dog

Finding the right basset hound requires some basset behavior on your part! You must become a determined hunter of just the right basset. You must get the correct mental picture of just what you are seeking and stay on the trail until you have found what you want.

There are many potential places to obtain a basset hound: newspaper classified ads in most cities that often have bassets listed, magazines like *Dog Fancy* and *Dog World* (See Useful Addresses and Literature, page 86) that have advertisements by basset kennels and breeders, and the Basset Club of America that can help you find basset breeders in your area.

Visit as many dog shows as you can. You can see bassets, and many other breeds, as they compete. You

will almost certainly be able to meet some basset fans at dog shows who will help you understand bassets and possibly help you in your search.

Most dog experts believe that in most circumstances you will have a better chance of finding the right dog if you go to breeders who have a reputation for quality. Buying a basset from the local newspaper classifieds is not unlike buying a used car from the same source—you may find just the right pet, but you may not. Breeders specialize in purebred dogs. They know that selling poor-quality, unhealthy, or defective dogs or pups will injure their credibility.

Male or Female?

Basset hounds of either sex usually make excellent pets. Males are somewhat harder to housebreak, but have a few more skills as early-warning watchdogs. Female bassets are a little smaller than males. They tend to be easier to train and housebreak. Unspayed females (see Spaying and Neutering, page 00) will go into season, or heat, approximately twice a year with the possible result of a litter of unwanted pups.

Whether you choose a male or a female is largely going to be your call. Both sexes have sweet dispositions. Both are good with children, but both are still trailing hounds that could wander away from home if not supervised or sufficiently fenced.

An Older Basset or a Puppy?

Adult bassets are very adaptable under most situations. One breeder said, "Many bassets feel right at home with whomever is feeding them." Problems arise with adult dogs when they have been mistreated, when they have not been properly trained, or when new owners have unreasonable expectations about bassets in general, and this basset in particular.

An unhousebroken kennel hound or a dog that was always outside in its previous existence may not adapt well to life in a small apartment. An overfed and obese urban house pet may not last long if suddenly thrust into the home of an avid rabbit hunter who wants the dog to vigorously hunt during rabbit season.

Common sense is especially important in choosing an adult dog of any breed. While bassets don't tend to have all the difficulties that some breeds do in living with new owners, they do need new homes where the owners understand the adjustment process.

Basset puppies are adorable. One problem facing the basset breed, as a whole, is the cuteness of basset puppies that contributes to impulse buyers who don't really understand bassets or basset owning.

Puppies require a great deal of time to help them learn what is expected of them. Basset puppies require special care in feeding so that they do not develop certain forms of lameness that afflict the breed. They also need to be kept from jumping, stair climbing, and too much exercise, all of which can cause young basset hounds physical problems.

Puppies are also moldable to what a family or an individual wants in a pet. They may require more attention at the beginning of their lives, but basset pups can grow with their families, which is a wonderful part of owning a pet. Basset puppies grow quickly, but they are also slow to mature.

Some adult bassets may be available from breeders. Some bassets are rescued from bad environments and may be available for adoption into a loving, knowledgeable, and responsible home. One can bypass many trying days of puppy ownership with an adult basset, but greater care must be taken to understand why the adult is available. Bad habits in an adult are

Only by careful research can an individual or a family discover whether a basset hound is the right choice. Potential basset owners should study books, watch breed videos, talk with basset breeders, and also assess their own personal hopes and expectations for a pet.

much harder to break than instilling correct habits in a puppy.

Pet, Show, Field Dog, or All Three?

That the basset usually makes an excellent pet to the right owner is well known, but it is also a fact that the basset has a good record in the show ring. Their original hunting role is still very much in evidence. There are AKC champion bassets that have done well in field trials and as rabbit dogs. Such versatility is not common in any breed, but the potential in many bassets is there.

Pet-quality puppies are those that have some cosmetic flaw that will not allow them to pursue a show dog career. These puppies, when healthy and genetically sound, are still prime candidates for those people who are

To keep your basset happy, with a smile on its face, you will need to be a consistent dog owner. Your responses to your basset's behavior must not waver.

Finding the right basset for you may not be an easy chore. Seeking the best possible puppy (or adult basset) to bring into your home will require research, study, and some hard work on your part.

seeking a pet basset. The price for such a puppy will be less than for puppies with show dog potential, but always beware of "bargain basement" bassets.

Show puppies are usually not readily for sale. Most litters bred by qualified breeders in most breeds may have only one really good show prospect, if they have any at all. Never expect to buy the top pup. Good prospects are rare enough to make them valuable in more ways than financially. Breeders will want to keep these puppies for themselves or have them in the hands of people who will show the youngster to the limit of its potential as an exhibition-quality show dog.

Carefully consider just what you want your basset to be, *before* you go out to buy one. If you aren't interested in showing or hunting with your basset, find the best pet-quality basset available that will serve as a pet and as a member of your family for the next decade and more.

Is the Basset Hound Right for You?

Before deciding on a basset hound, consider the following:

• Bassets are hounds. Expecting the alertness of one of the terrier breeds, the protectiveness of one of the guard dog breeds, the demand for affection and attention of one of the toy breeds, or the ease of training and versatility of one of the breeds that top the obedience trial title winners' list will only make you dissatisfied with a basset. To expect the basset to be more than a basset is patently unfair to the breed and to an individual dog.

• Bassets are much larger in length and breadth of body than most people realize. Their lack of height has made some people think of the basset as a small dog, which it most definitely is not!

• Bassets have such acute senses of smell that careful, extra thorough cleaning of urine or feces voided inside is *essential*. Dogs are instinctively driven to reuse elimination spots. If a keen scenting basset can find enough traces of former mistakes made on a carpet, it may decide that if this spot was good once, perhaps it will serve this purpose again.

• Bassets must be kept at home by sturdy fences and gates that correctly close and latch *each* time to avoid having the dog escape and get lost or even to be killed by an automobile while following an interesting scent.

• Basset puppies require extra help in growing up strong and fit. Though heavy in bone mass, young bassets shouldn't receive vitamin supplements unless prescribed by a veterinarian with experience in treating basset hounds.

• No dog should be simply tied or chained to a tree and left alone except at feeding time. While bassets do well in kennel arrangements with proper exercise, they won't do well chained or tied all their lives.

• Bassets are prone to obesity that can be torturous to their long spines. Feeding care is probably more important, with old or young bassets, than it is with most other dog breeds.

If you can fit such a breed into your lifestyle, providing for its needs and restraints, then the basset may be the right dog for you.

Are You Right for the Basset Hound?

Now consider these points to determine if you are the right person to own a basset hound:

• Do you want a basset hound as a fashion accessory or do you want a real dog with many good qualities as a pet?

• Have you owned other dogs that can serve as a reference point on how to treat a basset?

It is very important that you find out if you and the basset hound are right for each other. This sad-faced hound will only be what its genetic potential and its human interaction will allow it to be. Don't expect a basset hound to be anything other than what it is.

The source of your basset puppy is of greatest importance. Find a reputable breeder and see the pups' mother (and father, if possible) to get an idea of how these youngsters will look and act as adults.

Choosing a basset puppy should be the end of a long, careful search and the beginning of an interesting, exciting, and successful time for you and the basset!

- Are you so enamored with another type of dog that the laid-back nature of the basset will become a dissatisfaction?
- Are you willing to invest the time and money to search for and find the right basset for you and your family?
- Do you and your family have enough time and enough space to create the right environment for a basset?
- Are you willing to impress upon your family and guests that having a basset around requires that doors and gates be securely shut, no table scraps be given to the dog, and care be given in picking up this long-bodied breed?
- Will you, or another responsible adult, be able to stay at home the first few days after you obtain a basset puppy to help the newcomer settle in?
- Will you commit to regular veterinary visits for your basset? Are you willing to follow instructions about health care your basset may need throughout its life?

If you can honestly answer yes to these questions (and others that may be posed to you by basset breeders), you may be a suitable owner for the right basset.

Choosing a Basset Hound Puppy

You have carefully searched and found a reputable breeder who can give you a look at a litter of basset puppies. You and your family have discussed the sex of the puppy you want, whether you want a puppy with show potential or a pet puppy. You may have decided that you will want to field trial or hunt with your basset when it is older, and you have chosen a breeder who has produced bassets that have done well in these activities. You may have decided that you want a specific color. You have all the prerequisites charted out so that you can find a puppy that comes close to what you are seeking.

The only problem with this scenario is that it fails to consider the charm of young bassets. One couple was convinced that they wanted a red-and-white female puppy with some show potential and came home with a tricolor (black with white and brown) pet-quality, male puppy. The couple has been very happy with this fine pet but they do vow that their next basset will be a red-and-white female with show potential—probably.

If you don't want to consider other sexes, qualities, or colors, ask the breeder to show you only the ones that fit your specifications. You must decide that your specifications are more of a priority than seeing a puppy that really pulls at your heartstrings.

It is wise to look at several litters, if possible. Try hard not to choose a puppy from the first litter that you see. You may come back and buy this puppy, but give yourself the option of comparing as many pups (and their mothers, and their surroundings) as possible.

What Should You Expect?

You should expect to pay several hundred dollars for a good quality basset puppy. Show potential puppies could be as high as $1,000 or more. Different prices are the norm in different parts of the country, but you should always seek quality, and expect to pay a fair price for it.

Most reputable breeders will be as concerned about you as a potential owner of one of their puppies as you should be about them as the source of a puppy that will become a member of your family for (hopefully!) many years. If you have become friends with some basset breeders from dog shows during your search for the right basset, you might ask these breeders if they would say that you seem to be a good potential owner of a basset.

You also may want to see some references or records concerning the breeder from whom you are considering purchasing a puppy. Through this basset you and the breeder will be linked together for years to come and both of you should be content with the arrangement. Before choosing a basset puppy from any source you should have access to:

1. Health records, which will reflect all the information from any veterinary visits, what treatments have been given (and for what), and a dated listing of what vaccinations the pup has had.

2. The blue form that acknowledges that this puppy comes from a litter that has been duly registered as purebred with the American Kennel Club.

3. The puppy's pedigree or family tree, which shows its ancestry. The right breeder will have this pedigree and will be proud to point out the outstanding progenitors of your potential puppy.

4. Test results for the parents of this puppy concerning certain inheritable conditions. Chief among these is the result of screening for Canine Hip Dysplasia (CHD) (see page 73). These tests, and others are conducted on adult dogs and, while they are not conclusive guarantees that this puppy will be free from these ailments, parental test results are somewhat predictive in detecting the total genetic health of the mother and father of a specific puppy. The presence of such test results also is an indicator that this breeder has complied with accepted safeguards to assure the puppies you are seeing are as genetically healthy as it is reasonably possible to determine.

5. Other documents that a basset breeder may want to add, such as care and feeding hints, basset club names and addresses, and other items this breeder deems important.

What Should Be Expected of You?

Many reputable breeders won't let you buy a puppy unless they are sure of your fitness as a potential basset owner. To guarantee this fitness, there are some documents that a breeder may require of you!

1. A spay/neuter agreement for pet-quality puppies. Only the very best basset hounds should ever be allowed to be bred. If you have specifically designated that you want a pet puppy, a wise breeder will want to make certain that this puppy doesn't reproduce—a perfectly reasonable expectation. You will have to have a female spayed or a male neutered and show proof, signed by the attending veterinarian.

2. A return agreement that specifies that should your plans change and you can't keep your basset, the dog will be returned to the breeder instead of being disposed of in another manner, such as sold, given away, taken to an animal shelter, or euthanized. This agreement is at the option of the breeder, but the desire to maintain positive control over a basset that the breeder sold tells you a lot about the quality of the breeder you have chosen.

VIDEO LIBRARY
THE BASSET

Christmas puppies are a bad gift idea. Books, videos, and information about owning a basset hound puppy are excellent gifts that won't suffer during the happy chaos of the holidays, like a living gift can.

Note: An owner of a different breed found out that a puppy she sold was not being cared for properly. Using her copy of the return agreement, this tiny woman went and retrieved the now adult dog from the home of a famous prize fighter! Her responsibility went beyond the simple sale of a puppy.

Christmas Puppies

Everyone has seen or imagined a happy child on Christmas morning as it is surprised by a new puppy. This is, in reality, a most unhappy scene, at least for the puppy involved. Basset puppies need a lot of early care, socialization, and settling in to give them the best possible start in their new families. Christmas is a time of hustle and bustle in most households and a bewildered puppy can get lost in all the activity.

Unless the basset pup is the only gift given, wait until after Christmas to bring a new family member into your home. That doesn't mean that you can't buy books or videos about bassets to give as a gift foretelling the arrival of the puppy later.

Choose wisdom over sentimentality regarding Christmas puppies and surprise puppies given any time of the year. Basset hound puppies deserve to be cared for and prepared for to have the happiest possible outcome.

Spaying and Neutering

There are millions of unwanted dogs and puppies available today. Spaying your female basset or neutering your male basset is a sure way of not contributing to this glut of sadly surplus canines. Even if the breeder doesn't require it, unless you have a champion quality show or hunting basset, have it rendered unable to reproduce.

Many people feel they are depriving a pet of something wonderful when it is spayed or neutered, but that is all wrong! Bassets are not easy to breed. There are many problems that can arise in unspayed females, among them: twice-a-year seasons, tumors, false pregnancies, and unwanted litters. Males that are neutered will become better pets as they won't react to the scents of in-season bitches in your neighborhood.

Spaying and neutering is definitely a positive thing for you to do for your pet, yourself, and for the general world of dogs!

Your New Basset Hound Puppy

Before You Bring Your Basset Hound Home

The well-being of your new basset hound should be your first considerations. You have already begun this process when you honestly viewed the suitability of a basset as the right dog for you and your suitability as a basset owner. By taking a serious approach to preparing for the new basset in your life, you will greatly increase your chances of success as a basset owner and the dog's chances of being happy and safe with you.

Special Considerations for Basset Safety

Along with swimming problems that many bassets seem to have, the fact that the basset is built so low to the ground, has long trailing ears, and deep creases or wrinkles can also bring special safety considerations.

If you hunt with your basset or just take walks in the park, you should always be alert for broken glass, stinging or irritating insects, and other surface-level and injurious items that could cut a basset's ears or scrape its underside. Also check the mouth, tongue, jowls, and chin, areas that may be down almost on the ground when a basset is following a scent or just snuffling along.

Because of the deep wrinkles found in most bassets, not only should the dog be examined daily for allergies, rashes, and parasites, but the dog's facial skin should be checked for thorns, splinters, even sun exposure (especially in areas where the dog has white pigmentation on its face).

Bringing Your Basset Home

After you have safety checked your home and eliminated as many potential dangers as possible, you are able to bring your basset home. There are several important aspects to this first trip:

While this basset may have a worried look, it won't need to be concerned if its owner has taken all the necessary precautions to provide this puppy with a good, safe home.

Adults and children need to understand how to provide proper care for a basset hound. Not only does the young dog benefit greatly from this understanding, but parents and children have one more opportunity to work together toward a successful outcome.

1. Under most circumstances your basset needs to ride in the safety of a carrier whenever it is in an automobile but for the first trip home, a modification can be made to this rule. If your basset is a young puppy, you can let a responsible member of your household carefully and gently cradle the young basset in his or her arms. Be sure to include some old towels in case of motion sickness. This personal touch will help the bewildered puppy feel more comfortable as it starts its life with you.

2. When you arrive home with your new basset, put the pup on a leash and go immediately to the pre-selected relief spot. Wait there patiently until your puppy uses this area to urinate or defecate. Praise the youngster enthusiastically to make this natural activity a pleasant and memorable event. (To

aid in getting the idea across to your puppy what is supposed to take place goes on at this specific site, you could bring some urine-soaked bedding or feces from its first home to "salt" the location.)

3. After the pup has conducted its business you can then take it inside to begin making it feel at home with you. Don't let the youngster play too much—it has had a tiring trip.

4. At the first sign of the puppy getting tired, put it in its carrier. A blanket that has some scent from home will help the basset puppy identify with the carrier. You want to make certain that your pup identifies the crate with being tired and wanting to sleep.

5. Follow the same feeding schedule that the breeder used with the puppy, using the same food if at all possible.

The Adjustment Phase

A responsible adult will need to stay at home with the young basset for the first few days to see that the pup settles in and begins the adjustment to being in its new home with its new family.

The First Few Nights

The first few nights are usually the most difficult part of this adjustment time. Getting through these nights is crucial to the future success of this basset in your household. Many puppies will naturally miss their mother and littermates. They are in a strange place and this is frightening to them. When puppies are frightened they generally whimper and cry because this brought attention and comfort.

You and your family are now your basset puppy's family. When you place the pup in its crate for the night you, and every person in your home, must steel yourselves to the whimpers of the lonely puppy. What you do these first few nights can rarely be erased or undone. Your basset must learn to sleep in its crate without having to be comforted by some human from its new family. If you fail to teach your basset this key lesson, you may make the animal dependent on you every night for the rest of its life!

Your young basset will become comfortable in its crate after it comes to understand that this is its special place within your home. The first few nights the puppy will not be comfortable, but no member of your household can give in to feeling sorry for the pup, and holding it to stop its sorrow. Everyone must understand that a sad basset puppy that endures a few days of loneliness before it adapts is much to be preferred to a sad adult basset that cries every night. Dog pounds and animal shelters are full of dogs whose owners became exasperated because the pets never learned to sleep peacefully by themselves. Don't let your basset become just like them!

There are some things that you can put in the crate with your basset puppy that may help ease this temporary suffering. An old-fashioned hot water bottle, wrapped in a thick towel will provide a semblance of its mother's warmth. A nonelectric, ticking, old alarm clock can seem like her heartbeat. A radio placed near the crate or carrier, tuned to a talk station and on low volume can also be comforting to a puppy.

Place the puppy's crate not far from where you sleep but far enough that you aren't tempted to constantly talk to the puppy, and where the whining and crying won't keep you awake. Let the baby basset endure a few nights and it will learn that the crate is for sleep and it will rarely whine and cry again.

Be Consistent from the Start

Everything you do with the puppy should be consistent if it is to correctly learn what it has to do to please you. Owner inconsistency has ruined a mul-

One of the best investments for you and your basset is a cage/crate/carrier that will serve as your pet's "den" or own special place within your home. Such a purchase will also be an invaluable aid in housebreaking.

titude of dogs. If certain behavior is wrong one time, it should be wrong the next time. If one activity is permitted and then it isn't, dogs become confused and sometimes resentful. Set rules and standards of behavior and let these be the same each time. Your pup will learn much quicker this way.

The Cage/Crate/Carrier

Your basset hound will be a much better pet if you begin to crate train the youngster from the moment it comes to live with you. Crate training takes advantage of one of the greatest truths about canines, that they are denning creatures. Left on their own, all dogs will try to find some secluded area that can be rightfully their own place to sleep, relax, or simply be out of the way. The crate is just such a denning place for your basset.

Everyone in your home *must* understand that the carrier or crate is not a

Part of the denning instinct that virtually all canines have is a second instinct that is equally strong and equally natural. In the wild, canines are always careful to void away from where they have their den. Not only does this make the den a more pleasant place, it also keeps the smell of accumulated feces and urine from serving as a signal to other predators where the den is located. In your home your basset will want to avoid eliminating wastes in the place where it sleeps: its crate. This instinct makes crate training part of housebreaking.

Housebreaking

Even if your basset will sometimes stay outside, housebreaking your pet is a good idea. While it is true that bassets are not among the top breeds in ease of housebreaking, they can become housebroken with the help of a persistent and consistent owner. Here are some hints for making housebreaking your basset easier:

• Start immediately when you get home with the puppy to introduce it to the right place for it to urinate and defecate. Use the same location *each* time you take your puppy out to void. If your pup's relief area is a public area, always be responsible; clean up solid wastes and dispose of them appropriately. If the relief spot is in your yard, occasional tidying up will keep the area from being offensive to humans but will maintain the needed scent for your basset.

• Crate train your basset puppy and take advantage of the natural habit that most dogs have in wanting to keep their den area clean.

• Buy a crate that is large enough for the *adult* basset and then partition it off so that it fits the size of the growing puppy. Too much room in a crate may cause a puppy to subdivide and make one corner of the crate into a bathroom. Just enough room for the

This basset seems to be quite comfortable in its home. It is important that the house rules be made clear to a young basset, right from the first day.

cruel thing that is used to imprison your basset. Explain to each person that the carrier or crate is as natural for your pet as having a room of one's own is natural for human beings. Not only is crate training not cruel, it helps the basset puppy adjust to its new home, keeps it safe when the family must be away for a short while, and makes housebreaking much easier.

dog to turn around and to sleep comfortably is all the space required.

• *Always* praise your basset with lots of pats and hugs *each* time it does what you want it to do at the relief site. *Never* punish the puppy or dog at this important location; to do so will only confuse the pet and could undo some of the housebreaking lessons it has learned.

• Time your pup's meals with a trip outside. Young dogs have limited colon and bladder volume and taking food or water in generally means that some wastes will soon need to be going out.

• Take your puppy outside as late as possible at night and as early as possible the next morning. Don't be unintentionally cruel and leave a puppy with a full bladder in its crate longer than you absolutely have to.

• No matter how much you may want to housebreak your basset puppy, bladder control comes only with age. A young basset under one year old, and some over a year old, may not be able to keep from making messes now and then. Know that that is going to happen and be prepared to effectively clean up the messes and find some odor-covering agent to mask the latent smell in order to stop future repetitions at this same spot.

• When your puppy is out of its crate, watch it carefully. If the pup starts to look uncomfortable, comes to you in a plaintive manner, stays near the door, or starts circling or squatting, get it outside. Quickly and gently, and even if it has already begun to urinate or defecate, take the pup out to the relief spot and wait until it goes there, reward it with praise, and come back in.

• *Never* punish a puppy for making a mess. You can attempt to stop the act by firmly saying "*No*" or by clapping your hands to break its concentration as you go out to the relief spot. Rubbing a puppy's nose in its waste is

Becoming a good housepet, like this regal-looking basset, is not a matter of chance. Housebreaking is a chore with some male bassets, but a persistent and consistent owner can accomplish it.

stupid, pointless, cruel, and counterproductive. Your puppy won't even know why you are doing this. *Never* strike a puppy with anything, not even the proverbial rolled-up newspaper.

• To sum it up: Be consistent with your young basset. Don't change relief spots. Don't wait to clean up a mistake. Don't yell at the puppy. Always reward the pup for doing what it should at the relief site.

41

HOW-TO:
Basset Puppy-Proofing Your Home

Your new basset will need a safe environment in which to grow up and flourish. How you make your pup's living space safe depends largely on you and members of your household. Because of the low-profile stature of your basset, special care must be taken at basset level to remove any items or conditions that can hurt or kill your new canine family member.

It is important to remember that *every* area, inside and outside, to which your basset has access must be thoroughly checked for possible dangers. Here are some suggestions:

• Work from the bottom up. Get down on the floor and try to see dangers from where the basset lives, looking for things that could injure an innocent puppy or that it could swallow. Because owning a basset should be a family affair, enlist your children in the task of get-

There are dozens of everyday household items that can prove fatal to dogs and puppies. Seek out all of these items (and more) to create a non-toxic environment for your basset hound.

ting down on the floor looking for unsafe objects: sharp points at puppy-eye level and electrical outlets and extension cords that could bring instant death to a chewing puppy, etc.

• Stabilize or remove any heavy things that could fall and crush a young pup.

• Look for chemically treated areas where a young basset could come in contact with noxious fumes or substances. Cleaning fluid residues, lead-based paints on old woodwork or furniture, or forgotten ant or

rat poison could easily be ingested by an unknowing youngster.

• It is especially important that basset puppies *not* have access to steps, either going up or down. Trying to climb stairs and steps can do great damage to the developing skeletal systems of young basset hounds.

• Block off any balconies, porches, or hearths from which a puppy could fall.

• Close off any tight places behind television sets, heavy furniture, refrigerators, pianos, etc., that could trap a young basset that is only intent on following its nose.

• Eliminate access to any potential nooses that could catch a basset pup's head and cause strangulation in a frightened, struggling young dog. Some of these can be supports holding up railings, openings in trellises and fences, and other head-inviting gaps.

• Keep a basset away from household cleaners, detergents, chemicals, and other killers that are often kept in

To effectively puppy-proof your home you must get down to the eye and nose level of an inquisitive basset puppy. Only by taking this approach can a person see the hazards that exist in most homes.

Pins, needles, thumbtacks, even coins, can bring harm to a puppy. An integral part of puppy-proofing centers on finding and removing such dangers from your home.

cabinets and on low shelves, right at basset level.

• If your dog or puppy can get to your garage or other areas where your automobile is parked, be sure to thoroughly clean up spillages of gasoline and other fluids. *Especially* dangerous is antifreeze, which has a smell and taste that dogs seem to love, and which is a deadly poison to them.

• Outside there are many potential dangers down low where bassets live. Branches, edges, vents, wiring, and other items can be overlooked until your basset is injured by running into one of them.

• There are poisonous plants around many households. Some of these are azaleas, holly and its berries, milkweed, poison ivy, mistletoe, philodendron, jimsonweed, and other

regional wild, house, and garden plants.

• A preventive approach to basset-proofing is to crate-train your pet (see The Cage/Crate/Carrier, page 39) and then use the crate or an outside kennel

area for those times when your basset can't be adequately supervised or watched over.

• Be aware that swimming pools, decorative fish ponds, even large containers that can collect water can trap and drown a young puppy.

• For ease in housebreaking your young basset select a place where relief breaks can be conveniently and quickly handled. Always use this location to allow the scent of previous use help remind the young basset what it is supposed to do at this spot.

Most safety proofing is common sense, but by taking a carefully designed approach you will be less likely to overlook some danger. Prevention is always much easier than treatment or having a puppy killed by a lack of safe forethought.

Fenced yards, crates or carriers, and barriers to dangerous places within the home (stairs, landings, balconies, etc.) are all key elements in puppy-proofing where you and your basset puppy will live.

When housebreaking your basset, remember that lingering odors will entice your dog to repeat his mistake. Be sure to thoroughly eliminate all odors.

Paper Training

A less effective and less efficient way to housebreak is paper training. Because bassets, especially males, have more trouble becoming quickly housebroken, paper training may not be a very good alternative. However, it is the only option that can be used for basset owners, like those on upper floors in apartment buildings, who can't rush their pup quickly out to a relief site.

Paper training involves placing layers of newspapers all over the floor of some easily cleaned room like a laundry room or spare bathroom. Rather than having an outside elimination spot, the pup then has a relief room, or a relief spot in a room.

Paper training does work when a basset's owner must be away from home for several hours during the day, but paper training should always be only a substitute for the more effective outside method. Paper training breaks the rule against inconsistency in that sometimes it is okay to void wastes inside, but other times it should be done outside.

Layers of paper are used so that the top layers can be picked up, leaving a clean surface that still has a scent for the young basset to follow. Paper training doesn't work particularly well with the much preferred crate training approach. Taking a puppy out of its crate to another place inside the home can confuse the dog; still, paper training can work, to a degree, with some bassets.

The best way to view paper training is as a short-term partial solution. By establishing a relief spot in the room and gradually making that smaller and smaller until it can be moved outside, paper training can serve part of the housebreaking function.

Housebreaking your basset may take a little longer than with other breeds, but, with a little more patience, and with a lot of consistency it can be accomplished. Most basset experts firmly believe that all basset puppies can be eventually housebroken if the owner follows this patience and consistency model. Combined with crate training, basset housebreaking efforts aren't really much more difficult than most breeds in the hound group.

Training

All Dogs Deserve Training

That the basset is a usually calm and relaxed dog is true. That the basset cannot benefit from becoming trained is *not* true. All dogs need and deserve to be trained. There will surely be times in every basset's life when all that stands between the dog and danger is its training—leashes break; gates get left open. Bassets are still dogs and don't recognize all the possible dangers there are and good training gives a dog owner one more way to control his or her basset. Being able to control a powerful, though short, dog may someday save that dog's life.

Bassets are not the easiest dog for a beginner to train but dog training classes and the help of experienced basset breeders can make this task less difficult. Remember: Bassets are hounds and hounds are bred to chase things, either in a pack or independently. They generally learn by doing. Young hounds are usually paired with older dogs that know what they are chasing and how to do it. Other than coming back to their owners, many hounds, now and down through the centuries, never received a lot of extra training. None was usually required.

The top obedience dogs have almost always come from breeds that have to do jobs that require quite a bit of training. Retrievers and shepherds fill many of the top obedience spots because their jobs and their ancestors' jobs required them to understand fairly complex commands and behaviors. In a recent survey, the border collie was ranked as the smartest of all canines and on the other end was the Afghan hound, which was originally bred to chase something.

Hounds, and bassets in particular, are not "dumb" dogs; their lineage and activities require them to be smart in different ways from some other breeds. The bloodhound, the breed that many experts link closely with the basset in genetic heritage, is a rather good obedience dog. Bloodhounds have been trained in the very demanding task of finding fugitives and lost persons. Some basset breeders believe the basset could be developed to do the same job.

The Three Keys to Basset Training

The keys to training bassets are consistency, persistence, and patience.

A puppy's first trainer is its mother. From her a baby basset learns many lessons. Dog owners can also learn ways to get training points across by following a mother dog's example.

The average novice basset owner working with the average basset can use these three keys to achieve training success.

Consistency: A dog trainer who does a lesson differently each time has no consistency, and such a trainer will fail because dogs, especially bassets, need to clearly understand what is required of them. Without such clarity dogs become confused and possibly resentful.

Persistence: A dog trainer who gives up because training a basset isn't as easy as it looks in a book or on a video, lacks persistence. Training is a process, not a milestone. Bassets will need little refresher courses throughout their lives. A trainer lacking perseverance will never go quite far enough to get a lesson across to his or her basset.

Patience: A dog trainer without patience will never teach a basset anything, except possibly to fear or hate the trainer. An impatient trainer often lashes out at the student for the teacher's inability to teach. Bassets are loving pets and will usually want to please their owners. They don't *not* learn because they are obstinate. While they *can* be stubborn, that is where patience on the part of the trainer comes in. Without patience a basset owner is doomed to own an untrained and probably frustrated basset hound.

General Training Tips

In addition to the more specific keys to training bassets, there are several tips that can help with any dog. Some are the same for the basset, but are important enough to bear repeating:

• *Praise enthusiastically:* Your training role is to help your puppy achieve success and to be rewarded for that success. The best reward you can give your dog is praise. Some people use food as a reward, which may work

for them, but what do you do when you don't have any food and you want to reward your pup? Anyway, bassets don't need the extra food!

• *Correct fairly and immediately:* You want to get the desired response, not punish the puppy. A simple "*No*" or slight pressure on the lead and collar is enough. Immediate response is crucial; a puppy has a short attention span and later correction won't be associated with the misdeed.

• *Practice consistent repetition:* Your basset will need to have a clear understanding of just what you want. Give the command the same way each time and expect the same result.

• *NEVER lose your temper:* One angry outburst from you, directed at a bewildered puppy, could literally ruin this dog for any further training by giving it cause to fear you.

• *Be patient:* Already highlighted as a key for training bassets, patience is an important virtue in all aspects of dog ownership, but it is of greatest importance in training. The puppy isn't having trouble learning the commands to spite you—it simply may not understand what you want.

Pack Behavior

Basset hounds, and all other canines, are pack animals. Bassets were bred for their pack attributes for hundreds of years and trailing game in a pack with other bassets is as natural as breathing for most bassets. Pack behavior runs very strong in most scent hounds and is possibly strongest in bassets. Even wild dogs and wolves have a pack format to their lives. The pack forms the social hierarchy that controls most aspects of these canines' lives.

Once understood by a basset owner, pack behavior can be a great help in training a basset. The first concept in understanding pack behavior is that of the "alpha male." Usually the strongest and most dominant member of the pack, this alpha (for first) dog leads the pack in hunting, and therefore in surviving. This male will lead the pack away from danger, handle squabbles among pack members, and enforce pack rules. The alpha male get his share of the "perks" of leadership. He eats first and is usually the sire of the puppies or cubs born to pack females.

The second dog in the pack is designated as the "beta" dog and so forth down the line until the very old dogs and puppies are included. Each animal has its place and knows it. This is the glue that holds the pack together. Without a pack, survival becomes much more difficult for wolves or wild dogs.

Your basset will also have a pack. It consists of you and every other person in your household. It is crucial to understand that *every* human being *must* rank above the basset in the pack. In the worst case, a dog spots a vacuum in leadership at the alpha level and moves to fill it. In some breeds such a dog is truly dangerous, as it will do only what it wants to do and will try to remain in the alpha position.

Bassets are not overly aggressive and battling for leadership isn't usually their style. A dog that lives at your house still needs to understand its place in the pack. It is natural for a lower member to obey the higher members in the pack. Your understanding of this fact and filling the role of the alpha male sets the stage for effective training for your basset.

When to Start Training

Bassets are fairly slow to mature, with some maturing at different rates from others, even in the same litter. Some aspects of training have already begun for your basset. It has learned to sleep by itself in its crate, and it should also be housebroken. Depending on the level of maturity of your puppy, more formal lessons can begin after the pup is reasonably housebroken.

The Mother Dog as a Training Model

Even before you brought your basset puppy home it had received some excellent training by one of the best trainers possible, its mother. In keeping with the pack concept, and in keeping with the training tips, the mother is the leader of her pack of puppies. She enforces her will upon the baby bassets even before they have been weaned. She uses several tried-and-true methods that are good models for you to follow in your training.

Repetition: The mother basset made it clear to her pups that certain behavior would not be tolerated. Each time a puppy committed a misdeed, such as straying too far away from the whelping box, the act was met with immediate correction. The mother basset did this over and over until the puppies learned which acts got them punished.

Consistency: Already mentioned as a key, the mother dog is a perfect example of consistency. She didn't punish bad behavior one time and then reward it the next time. Her actions were identical each time.

Fairness: The mother basset corrects her puppies fairly. She doesn't resort to physical violence in enforcing her will on the puppies. A rough nudge from Mama is all the puppies usually need to make them behave.

Follow this training model and you will find training your basset is much less difficult because your puppy already knows how this model works.

Training Equipment

Several pieces of equipment will be needed for use in training your basset:

• You will need a chain training collar, available at pet supply stores. This collar is different from your basset's

The "choke" chain is not designed to choke or strangle a dog into doing what you want. It will provide the needed pressure to make your dog attentive to certain commands. Such training collars are just for training, not for regular use.

Bassets, like all other dogs, are really pack animals. Pack behavior and the hierarchy of the pack can be another aid in training your basset to become a good family member.

regular collar and should be used *only* for training purposes. When the young basset sees this collar in your hand it should realize that training time is here. This collar is often and falsely called a "choke" collar; used correctly, this collar does not choke a dog. When you exert slight pressure on the lead (or leash), this chain collar causes the dog's head to be pulled up with a gentle tug. This is to get and maintain your basset's attention so that it will be listening for the commands you are to give next. When used in conjunction with a firm (alpha male voice) "*No,*" your basset will know its actions are not to be repeated.

The chain collar should be large enough to go over your basset's head and ears with no more than an inch (2.5 cm) clearance. This collar *must* be removed after each training session is over. It is the training collar that should signal an end to play time and a beginning of training time and its impact would be lost if it became an everyday collar. Additionally, leaving this chain collar on a dog could result

in it snagging on something and either frightening the puppy or even possibly strangling it.

• You will also need a one-inch-wide (2.5 cm) lead or leash. This is a training lead and should not be used on regular walks and other outings. For a basset this lead should be constructed of leather, nylon, or woven web material and it should be six feet (1.8 m) long. It should have a comfortable hand loop on one end and a swivel snap, for attaching to the training collar, on the other end.

One trick used to help a young basset become accustomed to the weight and pressure of the training collar and the training lead is to allow the youngster to run around (under close supervision) in a room or a backyard with the collar on and the lead dragging along behind. Supervision will prevent the lead from catching on something and frightening the young basset.

It is important to successful training that the training collar and the training lead be associated in the dog's mind with the training classes. It is also important that the basset neither fear nor dislike either the collar or the lead.

Pre-training Hints

It is essential that you know how to correctly give the commands before you begin actual training:

1. *Be firm:* Give clear, one word commands to your pup, using the dog's name before each command to get its attention: "*Cleo, Sit.*" Use an alpha voice; don't clutter the command with any other words. This is training time, not play time.

2. *Be consistent:* Use the same tone of voice each time, so that your puppy will know by the sound of your voice as well as by the actual command that you mean business.

3. *Be specific:* Don't string commands: "*Cleo, come here and sit down.*" Each command should have a single, specific word. That word should be used each time in the same way to avoid confusing the dog.

Additional Hints
• Your basset will respond best if you do not allow any hidden agendas to creep into your voice. If you have had a bad day, don't try to train your dog. The tension in your voice will be conveyed to your puppy and it may believe it is at fault in some way. Training should be based on appropriate correction and praise, not on taking out one's hostilities on an innocent puppy.
• Keep lessons brief, no more than 15 minutes.
• Teach one command at a time. Don't go on to another command until your puppy has mastered the previous command. It may take several months for your basset to learn all of the commands, even longer in some cases. Let training be done in small, significant pieces rather than in a big, overdone, and often fruitless manner.
• When training time is over, don't immediately begin playing with your basset puppy. Put the puppy back in its crate and wait 20 minutes. This will separate training time from play time.
• Other members of your household should understand that training your basset puppy is important. They also need to understand the basics of each command so that they will not inadvertently undo your training when playing with the puppy.

The Five Basic Commands

Sit
The *sit* is a good command on which to begin because your basset already knows how to sit down. All you need to do is to teach it to sit when and where you say.
1. Begin with your basset wearing the training collar attached to the training lead.

Training your basset will require patience, but the finished product is well worth the wait and the effort.

2. Place the puppy on your left side next to your left leg. Hold the lead in your right hand.
3. In one *continuous* motion, gently pull the pup's head *up,* as you push its hindquarters *down* with your left hand.
4. As you do this, give the firm command: "*Sit.*"
When the puppy is in the sitting position, heap on the praise. Using the tip about continuous repetition, practice this command until your basset will sit without having its rear pushed down.
Warning: Remember the unique physique of the basset and *never* force the puppy down by overexerting pressure on its hindquarters! This could injure a young basset.

Sitting is something that your basset already knows how to do. As the trainer, your job is to teach your pet when and where to sit.

The stay is, at first, a bit difficult for some dogs, but persistence should make staying in one place (on command) something your basset hound will learn to do.

Keep training sessions on this command short. Don't leave the youngster in a *sit* long enough for it to become bored. As the pup improves in following this command, you can increase the length of time, always remembering to lavish praise on the basset *each* time it does the *sit* correctly.

The *sit* is of great importance as it is the command from which most other commands are begun. Make certain that you take enough time with your basset to ensure that it has mastered the *sit* before you move on to other commands.

Stay

Don't attempt the *stay* until your basset does really well on the *sit*. Without the *sit*, the *stay* cannot be taught. This command begins with your basset puppy in the sitting position on your left side. Initially, you may use the lead to keep the pup's head up, but the idea is to progress to a point where the lead isn't in your hand and you can walk away from the pup.

1. Using your basset's name, give the firm command: "*Stay.*"

2. As you give the command, step away from the dog (moving your right foot first), going forward.

3. At the same time you are giving the command and stepping away, bring the palm of your left hand down in front of your basset's face (*be careful not to unintentionally swat the dog on the nose!*) in an upside-down version of the police hand signal for "Stop."

All three parts of the command: the verbal, the stepping away, and the hand signal *must* be done simultaneously and the same way *each* time. This command will really need consistent repetition because it goes against a strong urge the puppy has to move when you move. Don't expect long *stays* at the beginning. Praise the puppy for *stays* of any length, but work to increase the time the dog remains seated.

If the puppy leaves the *stay*, simply go back to the starting point—the sitting position on the left—and start again. Do this several times, carefully doing the same things in the same tone of voice each time. If your basset puppy has some trouble with the *stay,* end each session with a few *sits* with the praise that goes with each *sit* so that your puppy can end each lesson on a positive.

Once your puppy remains in a *stay* as you walk away, you can introduce the release word *"Okay,"* given in a cheerful, upbeat tone. This will allow the puppy to leave the *stay* and come to you to get its customary reward of hearty praise for remaining in the position.

Heel

Once the puppy has mastered the *sit* and the *stay* and feels comfortable with the training collar and training lead, you can start teaching the *heel*. Begin with your pup in the *sit* position on your left, then:

1. Hold the lead in your right hand (controlling it with the left hand due to the shortness of the basset).

2. Step out with your left foot.

3. Give the firm command: *"Heel"* as your puppy starts to walk with you. As in all commands, use the dog's name to begin the command: *"Cleo, Heel."*

If your basset is inattentive or doesn't move out when you do, pop the slack of the lead loudly against the side of your leg (the equivalent of clapping your hands to get your pup's attention), repeating the command, and walking away all in the same motion.

When the basset puppy catches on to the fact that it should be walking along with you, give it some praise but do it as you walk along. Continue the praise as long as the basset is walking with you in the proper position on your left side.

Teaching your basset to heel will make walks much more pleasant. Rather than having your basset lagging behind, charging ahead, or twisting the leash around your legs, a well-trained dog will walk in place beside you, with or without the leash.

When you stop, give the *sit* command. Once your basset has mastered the *heel,* it will sit automatically when you stop. Don't let the puppy lag behind you, get ahead of you, or twist around to the other side. The purpose of this command is to get the dog to not only walk with you, but to walk with you in the right place and stop and go as you do. Your ultimate goal in the *heel* is to be able to get your basset to do it without the lead.

Never just drag your basset along. If the youngster has trouble with the *heel,* go back to the sitting position and start again. Gentle tugs will get your basset moving and keep it going. Eventually the *heel* will be part of your basset's command repertoire.

Down

The *down* begins in the *sit* and the *stay.* In the *down,* you won't use the upward pull of these commands, which is designed to keep the pup's head up.

The *down* is a *stay* with the dog's belly resting on the ground or floor.

1. Pull down on the lead with your right hand.

2. Make a ball-bouncing-like, downward motion with your left palm to convey to your puppy the direction you want it to go.

3. As you pull down and give the downward hand signal give the firm command: "*Down.*"

It is important that you don't use too much force to pull the basset's chest downward; that could easily injure the puppy's frontquarters. As with all the commands, the physical steps and the verbal command must be given at the same time so that the pup makes the connection that the downward pressure, the downward signal, and the command are all part of the same desired action on its part.

Once the puppy is down on its stomach, pour on the praise. Ultimately, this command should be fairly easy for the basset who doesn't have far to go to reach the required position. The goal is to have the puppy go into this position from the *sit* and then stay there until you release it to come to you.

Continue to practice the *down* with the *sit* and the *stay*. Consistency and persistence (through repetition) will usually teach a basset to go *down* and *stay* in that position.

Come

The *come* may seem to be an easy command, but bassets can sometimes be stubborn and may want to continue following some delicious smell they have discovered. There are several important elements to the *come* that aren't as necessary in the other basic commands. Rather than concentrating on your firm, authoritarian, alpha voice, let your genuine enthusiasm for the puppy show through as you give the command: "*Come.*"

Your basset will probably want to be with you anyway; therefore, this command is calling for the puppy to do what it already wants to do. It is important to make the *come* something the pup will obey immediately, as its life may someday depend on it!

At the beginning you may want to use your regular training lead, switching to a longer lead, one of 20 feet (6 m) or so to reinforce the idea that the command, "*Cleo, Come*" means *now*. no matter how far away the pup may be. You can gradually, gently, but firmly, tug on the lead to start the pup in your direction while you give the command.

The *come* is also different from the other commands in that it shouldn't be repeated over and over again in each session. Even with a praise reward each time the puppy obeys, a basset can become tired of continually being called to you over a short span of time. Use the *come* unex-

Training your basset to come when you call should be done in a happy and enthusiastic way. Never call your basset to you to scold or reprimand it for something. This will only teach the dog that the "come" command can sometimes have negative consequences. If correction is needed, you go to the dog!

pectedly in play sessions or when the basset is just walking around in the backyard. Always expect immediate obedience, just as the puppy should always expect to be praised for obeying.

A very important aspect of this command concerns *when* you call your basset and for *what* reasons. *Never* call your dog to you for something that the dog views as unpleasant: scoldings, baths (if the dog doesn't like them), and other negatives. Using this important command under these circumstances can be counterproductive. The *come* should be viewed by the puppy as a happy reuniting with the human it loves so much. Consistency in the use of this command is crucial. If a basset responds appropriately to your command, it should expect its customary reward, *not* a reprimand. If you have to correct the dog or do something that it doesn't like, *you go to the dog!* Don't ruin a good command by creating ambivalence in the dog's mind as to whether the *come* command should be obeyed.

Obedience Classes

If you have never trained a dog before, you may discover that you and your basset can get a great deal of assistance by attending local dog training classes. Not only are these classes usually taught by real training experts, they will give you a chance to mingle with other dog owners who are pretty much in the same position as you, and your basset can also become a little more socialized to other people and other dogs. You may be able to find out information about veterinarians, new products, foods, and other things you would otherwise miss out on.

If you have developed some friendships with more experienced basset people, ask them which training classes they recommend. Specific training questions or problems could also be mentioned to these breed experts who may have an answer for you.

Your Basset as a Field Trial or Hunting Dog

Not only does this versatile breed have what it takes to be an excellent companion and pet, win in tough competition in the conformation show ring, and show its smarts and training by capturing sought-after obedience titles, the basset can also be a more than competent field trial and hunting dog. Some people forget this breed was a widely acknowledged hunting hound for centuries before it won hearts as a pet and companion, won ribbons in the show ring, and won titles for its obedience work!

The basset hound is still an able competitor in the ages-old sport of tracking rabbits. While the beagle also has a great following in this popular endeavor, the basset has many admir-

Bassets, while a great pack hound, more often hunt in braces of two, or trios of three hounds. The leashes are usually taken off, allowing the bassets to follow a rabbit or hare trail at their own pace.

ers among the field trial set. Usually slower than the beagle or harrier (a breed of hound between the beagle and foxhound in size), the endurance and excellent scenting ability of the basset give it an edge in events where the winner needs staying power!

Basset hound field trials are regulated by several national dog organizations, the largest being the American Kennel Club (AKC). Trials are run in a variety of ways: with braces of two dogs, small packs, and large packs of bassets pursuing the wily rabbit through its natural habitat. Licensed field trial judges follow along, observing, evaluating the performance of each dog, and selecting the winning dog at the end of the trial. Trophies, fame, championship points, and acclaim from other field trialers are among the hard-sought prizes.

Bassets are also used as rabbit hunting dogs. Because of their slower speed and more deliberate style, bassets still have their advocates among hunters who want to be able to keep up with the dogs. Bassets, and basset-crosses, have been used on a variety of other game from pheasants to deer. In each instance, the scenting ability and the endurance of the basset have been among the attributes the hunters sought in their dogs.

In hunting and field trial events, the basset also brings another, more aesthetic quality—bassets have some of the most wonderful hound voices in all of dogdom! Their baying, especially in a pack, or on a track, is music to the ears of both experienced and neophyte hound admirers alike. Much like the voice of the large bloodhound, the voice of the basset has a ring of its own that brings visions of the centuries of this short hound's close association as a hunting companion for the gentry in France, England, and the early United States.

A Matter of Your Basset's Heritage

Bassets have been used as hunting hounds for hundreds of years. They were especially developed for this purpose and many bassets, even some AKC champions, can still handle field work very well.

Hunting with Your Basset

Using your basset as a hunting dog will allow you and the dog some exercise. Be sure that you are fully licensed as a hunter, that your basset has all its immunizations, and that the place where you are hunting is open land or that you have permission to hunt there.

Rabbit hunting generally allows one or more dogs to pick up the scent of the game, follow the game, and then turn the game so that it will run back past where you are waiting. Bassets do this very well but, unless you are an experienced hunter, go with someone who is until you feel at ease in this environment.

Be careful with your firearms and be certain of what you are shooting. Many novice hunters, shooting at the first sound they hear, have wounded or killed their dog or another human.

Added Care for a Field Dog

Field work exposes your basset to scratches, cuts, and abrasions that dogs don't get in their backyards. Be sure to carefully go over the basset, after you have returned home, for any injuries or parasites (see Ticks, page 71). Give special attention to the basset's underside, its ears, and eyes.

A hardworking field dog may need added nutrition if hunting is to be a common occurrence for you and your basset. You should also carry some drinking water to the field with you and a dish from which the basset can drink.

Large Packs

There are several kennels in the United States and other countries that regularly go to the field with large packs of bassets. This is an exciting event to see. Some hunts of this sort are by invitation only, but others will allow visitors.

Field Trialing with Your Basset

The American Kennel Club (AKC) has established a set of rules that pertain to bassets and field trials. Field trials are not for hunting rabbits; they are for grading a dog's capacity to track a rabbit. Many times basset events are held in large enclosures used for beagle field trials. These enclosures, often called running grounds, may be 20 or 30 acres inside of a sturdy fence designed to keep four-footed predators out and away from the population of rabbits that is maintained in each running ground.

A large group of bystanders will begin to march in a line through the running grounds, which are allowed to have high weeds and tall grass to make rabbits safe from owls and hawks. This line continues to go forward until a rabbit jumps up and starts running. The person who spots the rabbit yells "Tally-Ho." The spotter then points to the last place the rabbit was seen. Two or three bassets are brought to this spot and allowed to nose around until they pick up the rabbit's scent. When they have it they are released from their leads and judges walk along behind them to assess how faithful each dog is to following the exact trail that the rabbit took.

Hunting and field trial bassets are sometimes run in packs, but are also run in pairs, called braces. These bassets seem ready to do what the breed was originally bred to do—hunt!

Deductions are made when a dog loses the scent, has to backtrack, or gets on another scent. The basset with the least amount of mistakes is the winner of this particular run. If its score is high enough, this basset may be brought back to compete for the champion of the trial, second place, third place, and NBQ (Next Best Qualified).

While there are, as yet, relatively few basset trials, field trialing with beagles is one of the largest dog-participation activities in the United States. Basset trials are growing in number and afford some excellent fun for a dog and a dog owner.

Feeding Your Basset

The Importance of a Good Diet

All dogs need the right foods in order to thrive. Without the right foods, many dogs never reach their genetic potential. As important as any aspect of dog care, feeding is an often misunderstood and neglected subject. There are many opinions about which dog food is best, but all animal nutritionists acknowledge that a balanced diet is always the right thing for your dog.

In addition to balanced nutrition, there are three primary rules to follow in feeding your dog:

1. Find a high quality, nutritionally complete dog food and feed it *consistently*.

2. Don't feed your pet more than it really needs, even if it wants more.

3. *Never* feed table scraps, either mixed with regular dog food or as treats.

The Elements of a Balanced Diet

A balanced, nutritionally complete diet for dogs is composed of seven key elements: proteins, carbohydrates, fats, vitamins, minerals, good drinking water, and the knowledge and level of feeding consistency of the dog owner.

Proteins

Proteins provide your basset hound with the essential amino acids needed for growth, development of strong bones (so important to basset hounds) and muscles, and the continued health of these bones and muscles, and the healing of injured bones and muscles.

Proteins also promote the production of antibodies that help in fighting infection throughout the dog's body. Additionally, proteins are important in the production of enzymes and hormones so necessary for the ongoing chemical processes occurring inside your basset.

Carbohydrates

Carbohydrates and fats are the primary energy sources that keep dogs going. Carbohydrates are not as concentrated an energy source as are fats, but they are still a crucial part of the balanced canine diet.

Carbohydrates provide about half the energy as the same amount of fats would provide. For older dogs and

A basset will need balanced nutrition to give it a shiny coat and overall good health. Your basset will not *need extra treats, snacks, or table scraps, all of which can undo the best balanced dog food made.*

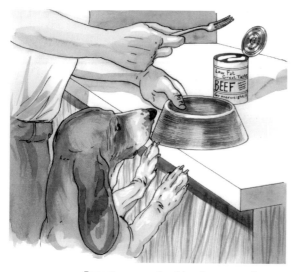

Basset owners should make every effort to learn about dog foods and the most appropriate ways to feed bassets of each age group. Feeding is often overlooked as an area of great significance in all breeds, but especially in bassets.

breeds like the basset that can easily become obese, carbohydrates are often used for lowered fat diets.

Fats

Not only do fats in a diet provide double the energy of carbohydrates, they also serve an important delivery service. It is through fats that the fat-soluble vitamins: A, D, E, and K can be used by your basset's body. Fats also help keep coats shiny and skin healthy.

Fats also play an important role in many dog foods; they make dog foods taste better. Foods that taste better (the concept is called palatability) are more likely to be eaten than are foods without sufficient fat content.

Vitamins

Another food-related area that is often misunderstood is the need for vitamins for dogs. Many people are so accustomed to taking vitamins themselves that they assume their dog should be on a vitamin program too. This is usually unnecessary, and it can even be harmful.

Modern premium dog foods are balanced and include all the vitamins that dogs need. The best way to provide vitamins for your basset hound is to find the right food and feed it consistently. Unless your basset-knowledgeable veterinarian urges you to give vitamins to your basset, do not give them.

Minerals

As is the case with vitamins, minerals can easily be overdone. Bassets have unique needs, needs that can be both met and harmed by supplementation. Discuss vitamins with your friends who are basset experts and with your basset-knowledgeable veterinarian. Most nutritionally complete and balanced dog foods are sufficient in the minerals dogs need. Unless you are given sound, expert advice to the contrary, leave minerals alone.

Water

One of the most important parts of good nutrition is plenty of pure, fresh drinking water. Water not only quenches a basset's thirst, it also plays a key role in respiration and in keeping the basset's system at safe temperature levels.

Clean water bowls regularly and keep them full of fresh, cool water. You wouldn't want to drink out of a foul-smelling, algae-ridden, slimy water bowl, and neither does your basset hound. When water is hot from sun exposure, dirty, or stale, dogs may not drink enough of it. Your basset can live a lot longer without food that it can without water.

Owner Knowledge and Consistency

Some dog owners don't consider what foods their dogs eat to be very important. They buy whatever product is on sale or whatever strikes their interest at a particular moment. Many people know more about cute dog food ads than they do about the dog foods these ads sell.

Without a quality food, a dog simply will not reach its potential. Poor quality, generic-type dog foods are made with less attention to the nutritional balance than to the bank balance. Cheap foods are made of cheap ingredients, processed in cheap ways, using cheap equipment. The result of such food being fed to a basset hound can be nothing else but cheap.

Dog owners need to know what goes into the foods their dog eats. They need to observe dog stools, which are a sure indicator of dog food quality (better foods are more digestible and the stools are generally smaller and firmer). Dog owners need to find a really good food and stay with it.

The best dog foods in the world won't work the way they are designed to if the person feeding them is inconsistent. The number of feedings, the amount of food per feeding, and the overall appearance of the dog being fed a specific food, should all be factored in by an aware dog owner.

Special Basset Dietary Concerns

Because they are the only large, short-legged dogs, bassets need special attention paid to their feeding. It is quite easy to overfeed a basset. Their appetites are generally very good and their sad expressions can practically beg for just a little more food in the bowl. Nevertheless obesity is one of the biggest killers of dogs. Bassets are not only killed by obesity, but they are crippled by the effects of too much

There is no more important aspect of basset ownership than that of correct feeding. Bassets can suffer, often greatly, from obesity which can rob them of years of healthy life.

weight on their elongated spines and on their hearts.

Bassets have a huge bone structure. They need a nutritionally complete and balanced diet to develop these bones. Too little quality nutrition can leave a basset spindly and unable to support its own weight. Too much nutrition can make a basset fat and lead to a host of problems. Talk with experienced basset breeders and basset-knowledgeable veterinarians about approaches they have taken in walking the line between too much food and not enough food.

Commercial Dog Foods

There are three main kinds of commercial dog foods: canned, semimoist, and dry. Each kind has certain advantages.

Canned

Canned dog food is the most palatable form of dog food. It also is the most expensive, most likely to produce loose and smelly stools, and most likely to promote obesity when it is overfed.

The "Spaniel bowl" is useful in keeping long basset ears out of the food and water. Bassets are normally enthusiastic eaters and they will want to become really involved with their food. Use of a special, high bowl will keep ears, not to mention walls, ceilings, and floors much cleaner.

Bassets that hunt, participate in field trial, or are on the circuit as show dogs will need more nutrition than will the average stay-at-home basset. In each case, keeping off extra weight is an ongoing challenge.

Canned foods, sometimes referred to as wet dog foods, are usually quite meaty and aromatic, which enhances their palatability. If a dog is started on canned food it is very difficult to ever get that dog to easily accept dry or semimoist foods.

Canned foods, which are from 75 to 85 percent moisture, can quickly spoil even at room temperature. Also, dogs fed exclusively on canned foods, which are softer than dry and somewhat softer than semimoist, tend to have more dental problems than dogs fed on crunchier foods, especially dry foods.

Advantages

• Canned dog foods have excellent shelf life if left unopened.

• They are convenient because they come in cans that can serve as one meal.

• They store better in the home than dry foods.

• They can be used as mixers with dry foods to improve palatability.

Semimoist

Semimoist foods generally come in foil or plastic-wrapped packaging in many meaty-looking forms. They have the convenience of canned foods without the high moisture content, thus there is less immediate spoilage.

Stool quality is somewhere between that of dry and that of canned foods, largely due to the 30 percent moisture rates of many semimoist products. Some of these products contain sugars and artificial colorings.

A great strength of semimoist foods is their portability and the fact that they can usually be resealed, making them excellent for trips and other times when a brief snack is all that is needed for the dog. The disadvantages of semimoist products are their cost and their potential, if fed exclusively, to contribute to overweight.

Dry

Dry dog foods are the most popular of the premium dog foods. They are also quite cost-effective, a point not lost on basset owners. They have the best digestibility rates of any dog foods and, because of this, they make kennel cleanup much easier.

Dry foods can make staving off obesity easier for basset owners because dry food can be fed in increasing smaller portions of less nutritional concentration than canned and semimoist products. Dry foods also keep well after being opened.

Palatability of many dry foods, which have a moisture rating of about 10 percent, isn't as good as it is for canned and semimoist products. Premium dry foods have made great strides in solving this taste problem. Dry foods have a lot of versatility. They can easily be mixed with other dry foods when changing from one food to another is desired. Dry foods can be moistened if need be, but canned foods cannot usually be dried out.

Dry food manufacturers point out that dry products with their crunchier form will help scrape tartar off a dog's teeth. While this may be true, no dry food should replace a regular dental care plan for your basset.

Scrap the Table Scraps

Table scraps are completely unacceptable for basset hounds. Bassets, possibly more than any other breed, need a well-balanced, nutritionally complete diet to avoid the crippling side effects of being overweight. Table scraps throw off the balance of a dog's diet, and because they are generally eaten with great vigor, these leftovers may cause a basset to not eat enough of its dog food, possibly resulting in nutritional deficiencies.

Some bassets are quite adept at begging for a little more food, or just another treat. Caution each member of the household that you can actually "kill a basset with kindness" by overfeeding it.

Older bassets, and dogs that have been spayed or neutered, need added attention to their diets. Because most bassets aren't particularly active, this group needs special diets that help keep them from putting on pounds.

61

Table scraps are the greatest contributor to life-threatening obesity in dogs. As a breed, the basset suffers greatly from being overweight. No table scraps ever!

Feeding Bassets at Different Ages

Feeding Young Basset Hounds (Under Two Years Old)

Feeding young bassets is a fairly complex matter. You have to provide enough nutrition for them to grow their massive bones and large-size bodies. You must also feed carefully enough so that the puppy doesn't grow faster than the capacity of its still pliable bones to support its weight. Rapid growth rates can result in developmental bone diseases.

There are a number of premium puppy foods available now that can help bassets grow, but do so at a rate that fits their skeletal development. Three of the largest premium dog food manufacturers in the United States have recently (1996) developed puppy foods designed specifically for larger breed pups, those

who may be over 55 pounds (22.7 kg) at maturity. While these foods were originally developed with "giant" breeds in mind—the Great Dane, the mastiff, the Saint Bernard, and others—it is reasonable to assume that bassets might also be good candidates for these special foods.

The way one feeds basset pups is very important. It is advisable for any first-time basset owner to discuss feeding bassets of all ages with experienced basset breeders, but especially the feeding of basset puppies during their formative time. Veterinarians who are familiar with the special needs of basset hounds may be able to recommend appropriate puppy foods.

Puppies should be fed four to six times each day, and should be fed only what they can finish during these mealtimes. Several feeding times are always preferable over one or two large feedings. Housebreaking is also much easier if you are controlling the pup's food intake.

Feed the same food that the breeder of your puppy was feeding before you brought the pup home. This will avoid the nutritional and gastrointestinal upsets that most dogs and puppies have when their diets are abruptly changed. Unless the breeder has been having problems with the ration he or she has been feeding, or if you can't get this food in your area, stick with the same food as long as it matches the needs of your basset puppy.

Feeding Adult Basset Hounds (Over Two Years Old)

When basset hounds have reached maturity their nutritional needs become somewhat different from those of rapidly growing puppies. Mature adults should be able to utilize what they eat and not begin to get fat. Some strains (families) of bassets may be more prone to obesity than others. Gauge how you feed adults by the specific needs of your basset and on the advice of the breeder from whom you bought the dog.

Adult dogs can get by with two feeding per day. These feedings should be as consistent as possible as to time, amount, place (within the home), and certainly the brand of food used. As with puppies, don't change brands of dog foods just to try something new.

Some bassets may mature slower than others. If your basset still appears to be developing at two years old, don't let some arbitrary number cause you to move a still-growing basset onto the adult basset plateau.

If your adult basset is a breeding animal, a show or obedience trial dog, or a hunting hound, the stresses and exercise of these endeavors may call for a little more nutrition, but even for active bassets, don't overdo it with food.

Feeding Older Basset Hounds (Five Years Old and Older)

Older bassets are the ones that usually start putting on weight. Feeding these older dogs requires that a great deal of attention be given to their needs and to prevent obesity. As dogs get older their metabolisms begin to slow down. They do less, therefore they need less food.

This is the age group that some basset owners begin to "kill with kindness." They just can't resist giving the old dog some morsel from the dinner table, or perhaps a little more dog food. Dog owners have been known to illogically say, "I always feed Cleo a full bowl of dog food and have since she was a puppy."

Unless you show real restraint in feeding an older basset, the risk is very great that obesity will become a problem with your dog. This is a terrible way for an older dog to have to exist. The added weight puts stress, sometimes great stress, on the old

dog's spine, joints, and heart. Obesity is preventable, but only if the dog owners prevent it.

Many premium dog food companies now make foods designed specifically for older dogs. Many of these are nutritionally balanced foods that have less fat than foods for younger dogs. Your basset breeder friends and your veterinarian can advise you about which of these brands might be right for your older basset.

Feeding Spayed and Neutered Basset Hounds

As previously discussed, bassets that have no future as breeding stock or show dogs should be spayed or neutered. Feeding spays and neuters is much like feeding older bassets. The accent is on preventing obesity by feeding a little less and walking a little longer for exercise. The same foods that are designed for adult or senior dogs can also serve well the spayed and neutered bassets.

Treats

Everyone likes to give his or her dog a treat now and then, but unfortunately, many treat items can upset the balance of a dog's diet. Some dog food manufacturers are now making dog biscuits that match the formulas of their various foods for different age dogs. These treats, given in moderation, should neither throw off the dog food's balance or contribute significantly to obesity.

It is quite easy to overdo treats. One basset hound owner noticed her older dog gaining weight so she immediately found a lower calorie food and began feeding that. Months later the basset was still getting fat. The owner discovered that each member of her family had fallen for the "Great Basset Scam" and had given the sad-looking oldster a treat every day, certain that one treat wouldn't hurt. Unfortunately, there

Treats can easily be overdone with the basset. Instead of giving in to those sad eyes and giving another fattening treat, try a flavored nylon or rubber chew toy instead.

were five members in this family, which meant five treats each day!

Home Cooking

Many experienced dog breeders believe they can make up a nutritionally complete and balanced diet for their dogs right in their own kitchen. Perhaps they can, but it is only their years of experience that diminishes the gravity of this mistake.

Dog food companies spend many millions of dollars each year in research to discover more and better ways to produce nutritional and balanced products. Unless you either have many years of experience or are a trained canine nutritionist, your home cooking will be very similar to table scraps, which should never be allowed near a basset!

Keeping Your Basset Hound Healthy

Special Health Concerns for Basset Hounds

Any time the form of a breed has moved too far from the natural wolf structure, the breed will have problems. The basset is just about as far from the wolf structure as any breed can be. Even with its unique appearance, the basset has relatively few inherited defects or physical problems. Some breeds have many more genetically determined concerns than do bassets.

Obesity

That great killer of dogs of most breeds, obesity, is the great crippler of long-bodied dogs like the basset. Their long spines just can't handle the strain of all that added weight. Proper feeding and exercise can help forestall or even eliminate obesity as a problem for your basset.

Von Willebrand's Disease

This inherited blood disorder is observed in as many as 15 percent of bassets. It is a hemophilia-like ailment that stems from an abnormality in the platelets in a dog's blood, which causes moderate to severe free bleeding.

Glaucoma and Other Eye Problems

Bassets as a breed seem to be genetically predisposed to glaucoma. Clinical signs are painful, bulging eyes. Other eye problems for bassets include entropion (inversion or turning in of the eyelids) and ectropion (excessively droopy lower eyelids).

Paneosteitis

Also known as transient lameness or wandering lameness, paneosteitis is an inflammation of the long bones in dogs from six months of age to two years. Thought to be worsened by stress, many young dogs (as do youngsters of other breeds with similar problems) simply outgrow it. Unfortunately, paneosteitis is sometimes misdiagnosed and surgery has been performed when the ailment is usually short-termed.

Paneosteitis is one of the reasons that experienced basset breeders don't encourage much exercise in very young bassets. Exercise can aggravate this condition and make it appear worse than it really is. Painkillers such as aspirin and cortisone have been known to offer some relief.

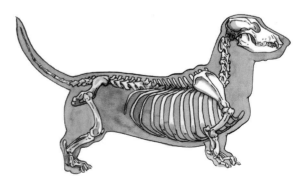

The basset is a strong-boned dog and needs appropriate nutrition.

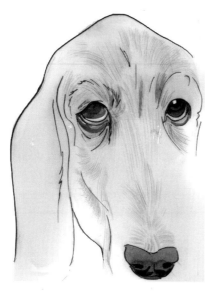

Glaucoma and some other eye ailments plague the basset breed. The drooping eyes should be examined daily for problems, abrasions, or foreign objects.

Allergies

Some bassets have a number of allergies, dermatitis, and seborrhea; the deep facial wrinkles cause these conditions to be more serious. The basset's long ears are also subject to skin problems and should be examined regularly and thoroughly cleaned with a mild cleanser.

Feet Problems

Not only are there possible skeletal problems in overweight bassets, but bassets are prone to interdigital (between the toes) infections and cysts.

Breeding Difficulties

Bassets' unique physiques make natural mating difficult for most bassets and impossible for some. Hand mating methods, where both the stud and the bitch are held in place for a mating, are practiced by many experienced basset breeders.

Preventing Health Problems

Your basset hound will depend on you for everything in its life: food, lodging, training, and other essentials. One of the most important areas of responsibility you have is the health of your basset. Because of the basset's unusual physical structure—a large dog on very short legs—a greater responsibility falls on you. A medium-size dog with average length legs will have enough problems, but a dog with a very long spine, an atypical canine front end, and the bad habit of wandering away from home will bring new challenges.

Preventing health problems is far better than treating health problems. Consider the following:

• The problem of the wandering basset can be stopped with good fences and better supervision.

• The spine and other basset characteristics will need attention paid to many aspects of basset life, such as avoiding obesity.

• Being certain that puppies don't injure themselves by ascending or descending stairs and steps is another way.

• Buying a good puppy from a kennel known for few genetic defects and inheritable problems is another way to ensure that your basset will have a better chance at staying healthy.

• A good, regular relationship with a veterinarian that has some understanding of the special problems of bassets will be a key part of your plan to prevent health problems.

• Experienced basset breeders who have "been there and done that" with bassets can share their own health care plans and even help you develop yours.

• Handle medical problems by taking serious concerns immediately to the veterinarian.

• Feed wisely and never overfeed.

• Read everything available to you about special basset maladies.

- Train your family to look out for the best interests of the health and safety of this shortest member of your family.

Immunize against Diseases

Veterinary medicine has come a long way in the past several decades. Diseases that once wiped out entire kennels are now rarely, if ever, seen in the United States. Today's basset has the best chance of going through its life without a serious illness as any basset has ever had. A solid immunization program, in the hands of skilled veterinarians, has made the expectation of a longer life for your basset very much a reality.

The first immunizations your basset should receive include distemper, parvovirus, hepatitis, leptospirosis, parainfluenza, and coronavirus. Your basset puppy should have received these shots at six weeks, others at eight weeks, and still others at twelve weeks.

Distemper

Distemper was once the greatest known threat to puppies and young dogs. Great kennels sometimes simply ceased to exist following a severe outbreak of distemper.

The immunization for distemper has struck a mighty blow in decreasing the incidence of this killer disease. Although still deadly in places without immunizations and in wild canine populations, distemper has been much less in evidence in recent decades.

Distemper is characterized by clinical signs that may appear as soon as a week after an unimmunized dog has come into contact with an animal with distemper. At first, distemper may look like a cold with a runny nose and a slight fever. Dogs with distemper will usually stop eating, become fatigued, listless, and suffer from diarrhea. Rush a pup with these clinical signs to the veterinarian!

Rabies

At one time stories of rabid animals roaming the countryside were the basis for many nightmares. The same thing is true today in many parts of the world, and in some places in the United States. Rabies became all the more frightening because it could be transferred to humans and by a once-loving family dog.

Rabies can afflict any warm-blooded mammal and is passed on through saliva usually conveyed by a bite. In some parts of this country, rabies is still widely spread among some populations of wild animals: foxes, raccoons, and others. An unimmunized dog that comes in contact with an animal with rabies can contract and spread the disease itself.

There are two forms of rabies: *furious* and *dumb*. In the furious form, the classical "mad dog" behavior is observed when an afflicted animal charges about biting anything and everything that it can get to, even trees or automobiles. Dumb rabies causes the animal to be almost sedentary with paralysis, unconsciousness, and finally death. Some victims of furious rabies die while in the furious stage; others go into the dumb stage and die.

Failure to keep your basset immunized against rabies is both negligent and unlawful. Make certain that rabies isn't one of the medical problems you have to be concerned about with your basset.

Leptospirosis

Leptospirosis is a bacterial disease that primarily damages the kidneys of a dog with the disease. In advanced cases, leptospirosis can also do harm to a dog's liver, and can produce mouth sores, jaundice, weight loss, and weakness in the dog's hindquarters.

Spread primarily by water contaminated by an animal with the disease, leptospirosis has several clinical signs:

In a young basset like this one, it is far easier to prevent health problems than it is to treat them. Regular veterinarian visits, the right food, avoiding stairs for very young pups, safeguards around the house—all of these can get a basset off to a good start.

Daily examinations and regular grooming will turn up most minor health problems. Special attention needs to be paid to eyes, ears, feet, and skin.

loss of appetite, fever, diarrhea, abdominal pain, and vomiting. Immunization and annual booster shots thereafter will keep your basset hound safe from leptospirosis.

Hepatitis

Infectious canine hepatitis is not the same disease that afflicts humans; this form can affect any canine and can progress from a mild infection to a deadly bout with the disease that can kill a dog within one day after it is diagnosed.

Spread by contact with the urine or feces of an affected animal, infectious canine hepatitis shows clinical signs that include listlessness, abdominal pain, tonsillitis, light sensitivity, fever, and bloody diarrhea or vomiting.

Annual boosters following an initial immunization will protect your basset from hepatitis.

Parvovirus

Young puppies are often the victims of parvovirus, but this viral disease can kill any unprotected dog at any age! This killer usually attacks a dog or puppy's immune system, gastrointestinal tract, heart, and bone marrow. Puppies often suffer from severe dehydration due to heavy vomiting and thin and bloody diarrhea. Within 48 hours from the onset of the disease, parvovirus can claim the life of its victim.

Immediate medical care can save some puppies with parvovirus. An effective immunization program can save even more puppies from this virus.

Parainfluenza

Parainfluenza is thought to be spread by *both* contact with an infected animal and by particles expelled in breathing and coughing from dogs with parainfluenza. Parainfluenza is highly contagious and can spread rapidly through an entire kennel, affecting all unimmunized dogs there.

Parainfluenza can be a cause of tracheobronchitis (with its dry, hacking cough and repeated efforts by the sick dog to cough up mucus.) Not usually a killer in and of itself, parainfluenza seriously weakens its victims to such an extent that they may fall prey to other infections and diseases.

Parainfluenza can bring on tracheobronchitis, which often has a fellow-traveler, *bordetella,* which is the most common bacteria isolated from dogs that have tracheobronchitis. This secondary ailment generally is found in tracheobronchitis' most serious form, bacterial bronchopneumonia. This whole group of intertwined illnesses can be prevented by immunization.

Coronavirus

Dogs of all ages can contract coronavirus, which is highly contagious. Clinical signs of this disease are soft or even runny stools up to very foul-smelling and watery diarrhea. Other signs include vomiting. While treatment can save a victim of coronavirus the dog or puppy is often left in a greatly weakened condition and open to other infections.

Other Diseases and Health Problems

Borelliosis (Lyme Disease)

This tick-borne disease affects many mammals, including human beings. Medically termed borelliosis, Lyme disease in humans is also called Lyme Arthritis. This is a serious and potentially fatal (more to you than to your dog) illness spread by the tiny deer tick (and possibly other ticks). Dogs and humans have come into contact with this ailment by being in tick-infested areas.

First diagnosed in Lyme, Connecticut, borelliosis is now found in every part of the United States. Once viewed as only a hunter's disease, borelliosis now has surfaced in city parks and

Fleas and ticks can make dogs miserable and deserve a basset owner's serious, immediate attention. Dogs that hunt or go for walks in wooded areas should always be inspected for ticks that could be carriers of Rocky Mountain spotted fever or Lyme disease.

other urban recreation areas, places where you and your basset hound might go.

Clinical signs of Lyme disease include tenderness around joints accompanied by swelling, and loss of appetite. If a tick bites you or your basset, or you find a tick in your clothing but no evident bite, seek immediate medical care. Have all ticks checked out by trained personnel. This is an ailment that can kill you. *Take no chances with any ticks.*

Anal Sac Impaction

The anal sacs lie on either side of the dog's anus. They excrete a strong-smelling fluid that is usually emptied by the regular action of the anus during defecation. If the anal sacs become clogged, the dog may be seen "scooting" across the floor or ground. Impacted or clogged sacs must be emptied by hand, by you (see page 23) or your veterinarian. Whoever does this less than appealing task will bring great comfort to the afflicted dog.

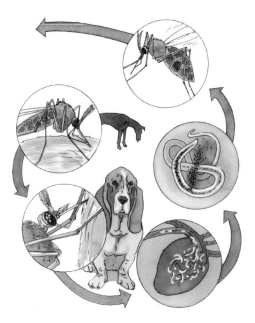

Mosquitos pass on heartworm larva from other animals already infected with heartworms. Untreated, these larva mature and can literally clog a dog's heart, producing great suffering and eventual death.

Diarrhea

Some diarrhea is common in dogs and puppies. It may be caused by changes in diet, stress, or by internal parasites. Diarrhea can also be a danger signal of the onset of a serious illness. Diarrhea that continues beyond 24 hours merits a trip to the veterinarian for your basset.

Vomiting

Like diarrhea, some vomiting is to be expected. For instance, excitement can bring on vomiting in a young puppy. Like diarrhea, food changes and stress can also cause vomiting.

It is also true of vomiting that it may be the first indicator of a more serious problem. Together, diarrhea and vomiting can quickly lead to dehydration, a serious condition in a puppy. Vomiting more than three times in a 24-hour period warrants a veterinary visit.

Parasites

External Parasites

Fleas: Fleas have plagued dogs since before history. They are the most common parasite affecting dogs and they actually survive by feeding on your dog's blood. In severe infestations, fleas can cause anemia and possibly fatal conditions for very young puppies.

These parasites have a parasite of their own that they pass on to their host, the dog—tapeworms that get into a dog's system through fleas (see page 72). Some dogs, like some people, have severe allergic reactions to flea bites. The flea bite allergy can cause severe scratching, hair loss, and great discomfort for the allergic dog. This allergic reaction requires immediate treatment by a veterinarian.

A flea infestation requires going to war against these parasites to get rid of them. This war must be fought on every front; anywhere that your basset can go or has gone can have fleas: your home, your yard, the doghouse and kennel, your car, your summer cottage, anywhere you went with your dog. Fleas leave multitudes of eggs everywhere that they can get to. Killing only the fleas on the dog is pointless if the dog is returned to an environment loaded with newly hatched fleas.

Consult your veterinarian or a pet products professional about the arsenal of anti-flea weapons you will need in this war, such as flea dips, flea shampoos, flea collars, flea dust, and similar products. Foggers, carpet sprays, and cleaners are for your home. Yard spray and kennel dust are designed to kill those fleas that live outside.

Fleas spend 90 percent of their life cycle *off* the dog. Only the adult fleas, about ten percent of the total flea population, are actually on your basset.

Ticks: Ticks are larger parasites than fleas, but they are easier to kill. Ticks gorge themselves on your dog's blood (or your blood) and greatly expand in size. Their bites are not only unsightly but can become infected and cause more serious conditions. Some ticks even carry potentially deadly diseases such as Lyme disease (see Borelliosis, page 69) or Rocky Mountain fever, both of which can affect dogs and humans.

Ticks can usually be eliminated with regular use of veterinarian-recommended sprays, dips, powders, and flea and tick collars. Your home and yard can be sprayed either by you or by a professional exterminator.

Ear mites: Your basset has long, hanging ears that create great hiding places for the pesky ear mite. These microscopic pests live both in the ear and the ear canal. You know ear mites are there when you see their dirty-looking, waxy, dark residue on the skin inside the ear.

Ear mites can make your basset very uncomfortable. If you see your dog violently shaking its head from side to side, or if the dog continually digs at or scratches at its ears, ear mites are the usual cause. See your veterinarian about how to handle these bothersome parasites.

Mange: There are two kinds of mange, both of which are caused by mites:

• **Demodectic,** or what was once called "red" mange is a problem for both very young and very old dogs. Demodectic mange causes rough and patchy-looking places around a dog or puppy's head, face, eyes, and throat. This mange can also cause widespread hair loss, and often quite painful itching.

• **Sarcoptic** mange is caused by a different mite from the mite that causes demodectic mange. The sarcoptic mange mite burrows into the skin. It

Fleas can carry a parasite of their own—the tapeworm—that is passed on when a flea-infested basset chews at and then swallows a flea. Bad enough on their own, fleas add to a dog's health problems by being an agent of introduction of tapeworms.

can cause severe hair loss and itching that can make the afflicted dog scratch itself until it bleeds. Transferable to humans, sarcoptic mange is usually short-lived on people, but it can cause a rash and some itching.

Consult with your veterinarian about what remedies are available to treat and prevent a recurrence of both kinds of mange.

Internal Parasites
Roundworms: Roundworms attack the health and vitality of dogs of all ages. These parasites are especially tough on young puppies that may have gotten infested by roundworms through their mother, even before they were born. If the mother has roundworms she will pass them on, which is a good reason for having all brood bitches dewormed before they are bred.

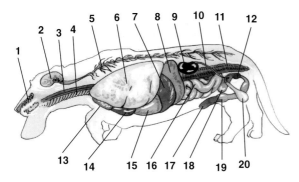

The internal organs of the male basset hound: 1. sinus cavity, 2. brain, 3. esophagus, 4. trachea, 5. spinal cord, 6. lungs, 7. stomach, 8. spleen, 9. kidney, 10. ureter, 11. rectum, 12. prostrate, 13. thymus, 14. heart, 15. liver, 16. jejunum, 17. penis and penis sheath, 18. bladder, 19. bulb, 20. testes.

Roundworms do much to sap the health from infested animals. Basset puppies that have a lot of growing to do in a short time don't need this further drag on their strength and ability to grow up healthy.

Your veterinarian will be able to rid dogs and puppies of roundworms, but you need to keep your kennel and surrounding area as clean as possible to avoid reinfestation. Remember that roundworms can also infest human beings!

Hookworms: Hookworms can infest dogs and puppies of all ages, but growing puppies are especially vulnerable to these little worms that are much like lamprey eels in that they attach themselves to the sides of a puppy's small intestine and drain off blood. Hookworms generally weaken a pup's ability to fight off infections and diseases.

Clinical signs of hookworms include bloody, tarlike stools. This parasite is definitely an immediate job for your veterinarian.

Tapeworms: Fleas introduce tapeworm larvae into a dog's system. Tapeworms aren't as life-robbing as some other worms, but they need to be eradicated by your veterinarian. They can sometimes grow quite long inside a host animal, and segments of tapeworms are sometimes seen in the stools of an infested animal.

Heartworms: Among the most dangerous internal parasites is the heartworm. Once a problem confined to the southern United States, heartworms are now found in much of the country.

The heartworm gains access into a dog's bloodstream through the bite of a mosquito that is a heartworm carrier. Once inside your basset hound, heartworm larvae begin to move toward the dog's heart. Unless they are eradicated, heartworms will ultimately clog the heart and kill the infected pet.

There are heartworm preventive medicines that must be started *before* a dog has heartworm larvae actually in its bloodstream. After a dog is infested, a serious, and potentially dangerous, treatment program must be undertaken to eradicate the heartworms. The uninfested animal can then be given the preventive medicine.

Ongoing Health Issues

Gastric Torsion (Bloat)

Gastric torsion, or bloat, is a very serious health problem for all deep-chested breeds, including the basset. Bloat can painfully take the life of an otherwise perfectly healthy dog within just a few hours. This condition involves a swelling and twisting (torsion) of the dog's stomach from water, gas, or both.

Just why bloat occurs is still relatively unknown. There are many suggested causes, but most experts believe that bloat may occur when certain conditions are present, such as:

72

- A large meal, particularly of dry dog food, followed by a large intake of water, followed by strenuous exercise.
- A genetic predisposition in some breeds (bassets' close kin, the bloodhound, is one of these) and even in some lineages within breeds.
- Stress from any of many sources, such as a severe electrical storm, for example.
- The age of the dog; a dog over 24 months old has an increased possibility of bloat.
- The sex of the dog; males seem to bloat more often than females.

In other words, a two-year-old, male basset from a family that has had several other members die of gastric torsion would seem to be a definite candidate for this condition. The clinical signs of gastric torsion are:

- Obvious abdominal pain and noticeable swelling of the abdomen.
- Excessive salivation and very rapid breathing.
- Pale, cool-to-the-touch skin on the gums and in the mouth.
- A dazed and "shocky" look.
- Repeated attempts by the dog to vomit, with nothing coming up.

Bloat is a true emergency. Alert your veterinarian and then immediately transport your basset to the clinic.

Canine Hip Dysplasia (CHD)

Canine hip dysplasia is among one of the most discussed subjects in the purebred dog world. It is a medical condition in which the hip joint is slack, or loose. This looseness is combined with a deformity of the socket of the hip and the ball-like femoral head joining the thighbone. This defective development of the hip and its connective tissues produces an unstable hip joint that results in a wobbly gait that clearly causes pain to the dog.

CHD is not always clearly caused by inheritable factors, but a smart basset buyer will try to obtain a puppy from parentage that is free of this disorder. The Orthopedic Foundation for Animals (OFA) has developed a widely used X-ray process that can often detect the presence of CHD. This test is best used in dogs over the age of two years. A new test, considered by many to be an improvement over OFA's X rays is the Penn-Hip test, which requires a specially trained veterinarian to conduct it.

Emergency Care for Your Basset Hound

If your basset should be injured there are some steps you can take to help the dog and not make matters worse:

- Remain calm. Dogs can always pick up heightened anxiety levels from their owners.
- Talk to the basset in calm, reassuring words, showing your confidence and radiating that confidence to your dog that you will make everything all right.
- Move slowly with no sudden motions or gestures that could alarm an already injured and frightened pet.
- Regardless of whether this dog is yours and has never tried to bite anyone, gently put a muzzle on the dog as a safety precaution. If a muzzle isn't available, a necktie, a belt, even a scarf can handle the job. Use caution using a muzzle on a dog that has been vomiting to protect against choking.
- After muzzling is completed, stop any bleeding immediately by pressure or by tourniquets.
- Move an injured dog *very* carefully in order to not make the injuries worse or hurt the dog unnecessarily. If you can get someone to help you, use a table or door or something sturdy to transport a heavy basset hound.
- If you have no help, maneuver the injured dog onto a tarpaulin, a blanket, or even a small rug. Slowly and gently drag this makeshift stretcher along to transportation to the veterinarian.

- Call your veterinarian before you leave your home or on your car phone, or have someone else call to alert him or her of your impending arrival and the nature of the injuries, if possible.
- Drive safely and sanely to the veterinarian's office and avoid putting an injured pet through two accidents in one day.

Giving Your Dog Medicine

One way to give your dog pills is to hide the medicine inside some treat. A more direct method is to open the basset's mouth, tilt its throat back just a little, placing the pill as far back on the dog's tongue as possible. Close the dog's mouth and wait for the basset to swallow.

Never throw a pill into a dog's mouth or tilt its head way back. This could result in the pill going into the dog's windpipe instead of down its throat. Give liquid medicine in much the same way, never tilting the head back very far. Simply pour the liquid medicine into the "pocket" formed by the corner of the dog's mouth. You can then tilt the head back just a small amount as you hold the mouth shut and rub the underside of the dog's throat until you are sure that it has swallowed the medicine.

Another hint about medicines: Don't give a dog human medicine and always implicitly follow your veterinarian's instruction of how much medication to give your dog and when. Always continue to give the medicine for as many days as you have medicine left.

Living a Good, Long Life

If you have taken good care of your basset, fed it correctly, provided enough exercise, taken it to the veterinarian on a regular basis, then you can expect that your long and short companion will be with you for 12 or more years.

Euthanasia

One day you will see your aged basset hound in a new way. The oldster has been a faithful companion. It may have helped you rear your children. You have probably walked thousands of miles together during your daily strolls over the years. You love the old dog and you know that it loves you, but then something changes.

There will come a day when your old basset can't move very well anymore. It will be in pain much of the time and will glance at you with those pleading, sad eyes asking you to make the pain go away, to make things be like they once were.

Because you can't turn back the calendar to a time when life was better and less hurtful for your old friend, you must make the most painful choice a dog owner must ever have to face. When is it enough? When do you steel yourself to say goodbye to your old basset, not for your sake but for its sake?

Your veterinarian can help you know the right time, but only you can make the terrible choice between bad and worse, between keeping this beloved old treasure with you even though its life is filled with pain, and letting the old dog go, marking an end to its suffering. Only you can know when to say goodbye.

Breeding and Raising Basset Hounds

Should You Breed Your Basset?

The only legitimate reason to bring more puppies into the world is to improve the breed. Bassets so excellent that they can improve the entire breed are quite rare. As a first-time basset owner, the chances of your owning one of these truly exceptional dogs are slim.

A word to the wise: Unless your basset is an AKC champion it probably isn't a good idea to breed it. You can buy another basset puppy for much less money than you will spend on breeding your dog to produce a litter of pet-quality puppies.

Before you decide to breed your basset, visit a local animal shelter. Look at all the puppies and older dogs for adoption. Realize that if one out of ten of them is adopted (which is about average for many shelters), that nine out of ten meets some other fate. Unless you have gone to a shelter that specializes in not killing surplus canines, you know exactly what the fate of 90 percent of those dogs and puppies was. Do you want to bring more puppies onto the scene to knock out the chances of a doomed pup being adopted?

Your Responsibilities as a Dog Breeder

To be a truly responsible breeder of purebred dogs you should take the attitude that you are responsible, *for life*, for any puppies you cause to be born. That means that you will keep any unsold puppies for as long as they live,

if you can't find good homes for them. That also means that you will take back any bassets that don't work out in the homes where you placed them.

Bassets Aren't Easy to Breed

Due to their unique anatomy, bassets don't breed well without human intervention. If all bassets had to depend on their own abilities to reproduce, it is possible that the breed might die out over time.

Humans have to hold both the male and the female in order for them to

Before you decide to breed dogs of any breed, go to an animal shelter and see for yourself about the canine surplus. Imagine that there are thousands of such shelters and millions of such puppies and dogs, most of which will not *be adopted.*

Allowing a litter of basset puppies to be born should signify that the breeder of these puppies will undertake a serious responsibility for each puppy throughout that pup's entire life.

mate to produce a litter of puppies. Only human supervision accounts for the number of little bassets that are available.

The Female Basset Hound

To be considered worthy of the title of brood bitch, a female basset must be truly exceptional. She must have good conformation, hopefully certified by her AKC championship. She must have an excellent temperament, which isn't so difficult in bassets. She must be healthy and veterinarian-checked as to her physical capability to be a mother.

Her pedigree must be compatible with the excellent stud dog that has been chosen to be sire of her puppies. Her lineage must be as free as possible of any inheritable diseases.

The Male Basset Hound

The ideal basset hound stud dog will be a top show dog that has also proven his worth, many times over, as a sire of excellent puppies. This stud should be one of the top male bassets in the United States and will command a good stud fee and possibly the "pick" of all his litters.

He should be free from any behavioral or physical problems and his pedigree should fit well with the brood bitch that he is to mate with.

When to Breed

A female basset hound will normally come into season (or heat) approximately every six months. This is called the estrous cycle and there are several phases:

Proestrus, or the preparation part of the cycle, is marked by the onset of activity in the uterus and in the ovaries. The ovaries are producing eggs (ova). As these eggs mature, the uterus thickens and a blood-tinged vaginal discharge is observable. Proestrus lasts an average of nine days (but could be as short as four days or as long as two weeks). During proestrus a female can attract males, but she is not ready to mate with them. Additionally, the vulva (external female genitalia) will begin to swell during the proestrus phase.

Estrus is the second phase of the estrous cycle. Estrus comes close behind proestrus. In estrus, the vaginal discharge loses its bloody tinge as it takes on a clear color and a thick, mucuslike consistency. Males continue to be attracted to this female and mating can take place during estrus. Ovulation occurs during this phase and usually happens between the ninth day (from the start of the estrous cycle) and the fourteenth day. Estrus will last approximately the same length of time as did proestrus, with pregnancy possible during the entire estrus phase.

Metestrus (or diestrus) occurs if your basset bitch has mated during the estrus phase. Metestrus will continue for the next six to eight weeks as the female's body undergoes changes that will make her able to bear and care for her upcoming litter.

Anestrus, the last phase of the estrous cycle, starts as metestrus ends, when the female's body goes back to the way it was before she became pregnant. Her uterus and ovaries will go back to their normal noncycle form.

If this basset bitch did *not* mate during this cycle she will gradually go "out of heat" with a resultant shrinking in size of her vulva, cessation of vaginal discharge, and the return of ovarian inactivity. This nonphase will last until she goes into heat again in about five months.

Your basset bitch should not be allowed to mate until her third regular heat at approximately 20 months of age.

During the entire estrous cycle your female should be kept strictly away from all male dogs. This means keeping her out of sight and out of circulation. A simple fence will not deter ardent suitors intent on romance. Unless you want an unplanned litter you will need to make careful plans to safeguard your bitch.

Mating

Most breeders try to put the stud dog with an ovulating bitch on the ninth day of the estrous cycle. Bassets don't do well in the "let Nature take its course" method of dog breeding. Both the stud and the bitch will have to be restrained to make mating possible. The stud will need help in guiding his penis into the bitch's vagina.

Some basset females will fight the stud dogs during mating; therefore, both dogs need to be protected from any hostilities that might occur.

When dogs copulate, they normally become "tied" or locked together by the effect of the interaction between the penis and the vagina. Mating should cease in less than 20 minutes. It is possible that a male and female

Bassets need to be given as much human contact as possible. This youngster is quite content to be squarely between the feet of its human.

could mate more than once during the two days of the estrous cycle of maximum receptiveness.

Pregnancy

Usually a female that has mated with a male and conceived will have a gestation period of about 63 days. In her sixth week of pregnancy, your female will begin to really look like a brood matron. Not only has her abdomen become swollen, but her teats are enlarged in order to be ready to feed her soon-to-be hungry litter.

Basset puppies are usually quite easy to socialize. It is helpful, however, to make sure that the pups meet as many types of people as possible to help them adjust to their new worlds.

The Whelping Box and Kit

Prepare thoroughly and early for the arrival of the new puppies. Don't let a premature delivery catch you off guard. One special need is for a whelping box. This is important as a place for the puppies to be born and raised for the first few weeks of their lives.

There are some excellent models to follow in constructing a whelping box, but you might do well to consider buying one of the manufactured whelping boxes made of coated, heavy-duty fiberboard. Most of these contain the all-important inside shelf that prevents a newborn puppy from being crushed or smothered by its mother as she lies down in the box.

Be sure whatever you use for a whelping box is large enough for the mother basset to be comfortable when stretched out and lying on her side. She will not only be having her pups in this box, but she will be nursing them there for a few weeks.

The whelping box should be placed away from drafts and out of heavily traveled areas. The location of the box needs to be warm, dry, and quiet. The floor of the whelping box should be covered with several layers of newspaper or with blank newsprint, if available. This will allow a layer of soiled paper to be removed without having to completely disrupt the mother and puppies.

A whelping kit, with all the things you will need to help with the birth, should be assembled well in advance. Some of the things you may want in this kit (or nearby) are:

• A telephone and the numbers of some experienced basset breeders and your veterinarian.

• Heavy surgical thread, or dental floss, with a pair of sharp-edged, sterilized scissors, to first tie off, and then cut the puppies' umbilical cords.

• Some clean and absorbent toweling.

Always treat a pregnant female with a great deal of care and gentleness, most especially if this is her first litter. Try to understand the changes she is going through and why she might be bewildered at everything.

With bassets, as with most dogs, the weight gain experienced by a pregnant female should be from her fast-developing litter and not from too much fat. A fat brood bitch may have trouble whelping her pups. Feed her a highly nutritious dog food, but avoid overfeeding her.

About two weeks before the puppies are expected you should place the mother-to-be away from any other dogs that you may have. Put her where she is away from any stress, small children, or any strenuous activities. Keep her as quiet as possible and cater to her needs. She needs your support at this time.

- A towel-lined, heated box (85 to 90°F [29.4–32.2°C]) for early arrivals to keep them warm as their siblings are being born.
- An emergency puppy-nursing kit with some milk replacer formula.

Whelping

If this is your first whelping you may want to ask an experienced basset breeder to help you. If your basset is likely to have any trouble at all, it would be wise to take her to the veterinarian's office well in advance of the actual time for whelping.

Normally your mother basset will have no problem birthing or caring for her new babies. She will usually pull away the birth sac and bite through the umbilical cords. She will then nudge the newborn toward her bulging teats for a warm first meal of the all-important colostrum, which not only serves as food, but as a temporary way to share the mother's immunities to many diseases.

Always move slowly and deliberately around your mother basset. She is normally a calm and placid dog, but you don't want to add any stress by herky-jerky movements or loud talking. Speak slowly and reassuringly to her as you place her first puppies in the heated box. Watch for some afterbirth to be expelled after each puppy is born. If you believe she has retained some afterbirth after the last puppy has been born, call your veterinarian, who may advise you to bring the mother and puppies into the clinic.

Care of the Puppies

The room you have chosen as the place for the whelping box should be kept at a constant temperature level between 80 and 85°F (26.7–29.4°C). Newborn puppies cannot tolerate great ranges in temperature. Their mother will keep them as warm as she can, but you need to avoid any danger of chilling these vulnerable newborn basset puppies.

Keep this room out of bounds for visitors for the first few days after whelping. The mother basset may be tense in the presence of strangers or a large number of people so don't add to her stress by showing off her babies too early. She will normally take excellent care of her new litter but her attention needs to be focused on her offspring and not on outside interruptions.

If the mother dog dies or shows no interest in her puppies, you will have to become their surrogate mother. These hungry little bassets will need to be fed a rich bottled formula (approved by your veterinarian) every four hours for their first month. Feeding them will become the big thing in your life for that month because hungry puppies will let you know when you are even a few minutes behind schedule.

When your puppies are six weeks old they should get their first round of immunizations (see Immunize against Diseases, page 67). Your veterinarian can also deworm them at this time.

Weaning

You can assist the mother basset in weaning her puppies by gradually introducing them to dampened, but not soggy, premium dry puppy food. Let some crumbs of this moist food get on your fingers and allow these baby hounds to smell them and lick the food off. Gradually let them have some moist puppy food of their own (don't let their mother eat it all). By the time they are weaned they should be readily eating the puppy food from a large, low, not-easily-turned-over feeding pan.

Finding Good Homes

When your puppies are about seven weeks old they will be ready for new homes. You are now in a reverse position from the time when you were

The goal of everyone who attempts to breed dogs should be to produce the best dogs possible and then to find each litter member the best home possible.

trying to convince a basset breeder that you were a good choice to own one of his or her puppies. People will be coming to *you* now and trying to convince you of the same thing. Be very selective and strive to get the very best homes available for each pup in this litter you have allowed to be born. Remember that you may have to keep some of these bassets until such a home comes along, and forever if it doesn't.

Bassets and Other Hounds

The Scent Hound Heritage

Hounds make up one of the largest groups of dogs in most registries. Throughout the world, there are many more hound breeds than terriers, herding dogs, and other working breeds. Hounds are generally quite specialized, which is especially true of the scent hounds.

There are two kinds of hounds: *scent* hounds that follow or trail game with their keen scenting abilities and *sight* hounds (also called gazehounds). Bassets, bloodhounds, foxhounds and beagles are among the scent hounds. Afghans, greyhounds, whippets, borzois, and Irish wolfhounds are among sight hound breeds.

Just as many fast horse breeds can trace their lineage to the Arabian breed of horses, so can many scent hound breeds trace their beginnings to the Saint Hubert hound, the near ancestor of both the basset and the bloodhound. Many hound breeds look somewhat different from this early progenitor, the Saint Hubert, which resembled the bloodhound, but all of them gained scenting ability or "nose" from this ancient genetic wellspring.

Understanding Hounds

To understand the basset it is important to understand the basset's place in the pantheon of hound breeds. Even if a basset is meant to only be a family pet, there are many hound aspects that must be taken into account regarding this dog. One such aspect has been mentioned throughout this book: The basset likes to follow its nose on a trail and can get lost doing so, thus requiring constant supervision or good fencing. This is part of the basset's hound heritage.

All scent hound breeds tend to be highly specialized (the otterhound is an example). The game for which a hound breed has been developed will often dictate the appearance of the breed and other characteristics. For example, a foxhound will need speed where a basset will need a better nose and endurance. Understanding various hound breeds helps show how the basset developed as it did.

This handsome trio of bassets are members of one of the oldest of scent hound breeds, the basset hound. After years of being relegated to pet status, many people are beginning to recognize the basset for its hunting abilities.

Bassets are scent hounds. Some other scent hounds are, left to right: the English foxhound, the American foxhound, the bloodhound, the basset hound, the otterhound, the beagle, and the harrier.

Bloodhounds

The bloodhound is a near cousin of the basset. Except for the added height of the bloodhound, and the basset's front leg structure, the two breeds are quite similar in most other ways. The bloodhound was developed to be a slow and careful trailer of large game, and later human beings. The basset hound was developed to be a slow and careful trailer of rabbits and hares. In form and structure, as well as scenting ability, it took on many bloodhound attributes. Longer legs were not needed for rabbit hunting so the early basset breeders didn't add them to the breed's physical package.

Beagles

Beagles and bassets share the same game, the rabbit. It is there that much of the resemblance stops. Bassets are slow and plodding, beagles are usually quicker and more agile. Beagles trail over much of the same kind of terrain as do bassets, but they have longer legs and smaller bodies.

Beagles, like bassets, are one of the hound breeds that have become popular family pets. They are generally sweet-natured like bassets, but are much more active.

English Foxhounds

These are the "talley-ho" dogs that British aristocracy and well-heeled Americans often follow on horseback over fences and hedges. English foxhounds are usually pack dogs, as many hunting bassets were and are. They are bred especially for the chase of the fox.

English foxhounds provided genetic material in most of American hound breeds, but there is no record of bassets having any foxhound forebearers.

American Foxhounds

Known to many Americans only through the book (by McKinley Kantor) *The Voice of Bugle Ann* and the movie of the same name, starring the late Lionel Barrymore, American foxhounds are a little taller and a little lighter than their English kin.

While some are followed on horseback, most American foxhounds are followed by the ear of grateful listeners, who find the baying (barking) of these hounds to be very pleasant and nostalgic. Many American foxhounds hunt coyotes as well as foxes. In some parts of the country, foxhound packs run in fenced and stocked enclosures, some covering many hundreds of acres.

Harriers

Somewhat smaller than the fox-hound and somewhat larger than the beagle, the harrier is a product of crossing both breeds. They are faster hunters used for hares that are usually quicker and larger than native American rabbits.

Harriers are now fairly rare, but they are still seen at dog shows. One sees more harriers, as the name implies, in areas where snowshoe hares are found.

Coonhounds

Coonhounds are bred to chase and then tree one of the wiliest of all American game animals, the rac-coon. There are several kinds of coonhounds: the bluetick (a black-and-white spotted/ticked breed); the redbone (an all-red, slightly smaller hound); the "English" coonhound, which is a color variation on the blue-tick; the treeing Walker, which is a coonhound as opposed to the "run-ning" Walker, which is an American foxhound; the Plott, a big, often brindle hound, which is also used to hunt big game (mountain lions, bears, wild boars); and the black-and-tan coonhound, which is the only coon-hound registered with the American Kennel Club. The other coonhound breeds are registered with the United Kennel Club.

Otter Hounds

The otter hound, now one of the rarest breeds of purebred dogs in the world, is much like a bloodhound with a rough, wiry coat. This helped protect the otter hound from the rigors of pur-suing the powerful otter in cold water.

Griffon Vendeens and Basset Griffon Vendeens

The French have for centuries pro-duced many unique hound breeds. The griffon vendeens are longer-haired versions of the general types of hounds already discussed. The grand griffon vendeen is roughly the equiva-lent of the foxhound; the Briquet grif-fon vendeen fits the harrier role.

Among French *bas* or low-set hounds are the basset griffon vendeens, grande (large) and petite (small). These "bassets" are low-set, but without the apparent heaviness of the basset hounds. The larger version is rarely seen in the United States while the petit basset griffon vendeen has recently achieved considerable popularity as a show dog and pet. Referred to by its initials, the PBGV is a small basset with a rough, almost wiry coat. Like the basset hound, the PBGV has great appeal and attracts much attention. The PBGV has less of the basset's calm nature and seems more of a "life-of-the-party" type of dog.

Artesian Normand Basset

This French breed, not seen in the United States, is a close relative of the basset hound. The Artesian Normand could be described as a basset hound with less wrinkling, and a more active metabolism.

Bassets and Dachshunds

While dachshunds are not techni-cally hounds (*hund* means "dog" in German), they do belong with any dis-cussion of basset hounds and other breeds. Possessing the same long and low body structure, both breeds face some of the same bone structure and obesity problems, but in many other areas, the breeds are quite different.

The basset is almost phlegmatic and the dachshund is more terrierlike. The basset is a long, low dog with lots of

This young basset could be sniffing to catch a scent of a cottontail rabbit or a snowshoe hare, but then again this pup could be catching all those good smells from the cookout on the next block.

generally is), is bred in only one size and has only one type of coat that comes in every known hound color. There are two sizes of dachshunds—miniature and standard—and three coats—smooth, wirehaired, and long-haired. Dachshunds are bred in only a few colors with solid red and black-and-tan being the most popular.

The Cost of Comparison

If the basset is seen only as a hunting hound, it could be surpassed by taller, swifter hounds. The basset, the beagle, and, to a lesser extent, the bloodhound and the PBGV, have transcended the boundaries of usual scent hound activities. They have become recognized for their pet qualities.

Many of the other hound breeds are rare; some are facing extinction. Others are relegated only to their hunting duties. It is probable that the basset hound would be much less popular if hunting were its sole attraction as the year 2000 approaches. Hunting is now an avocation for a vast majority of hunters, not a vocation that survival depends on. The basset, still a hound with all that the name implies, has made the transition.

extra skin, long ears, and wrinkles. The dachshund is long and low with tight skin and unhoundlike ears.

The basset, if the PBGV is regarded as a totally separate breed (which it

This basset has perfected looking sad, one of the breed's most appealing attributes. Responsible basset owners will keep this success just a facial expression by giving their pet the best of care.

Useful Addresses and Literature

Organizations
American Kennel Club
51 Madison Avenue
New York, NY 10038
(212) 696-8200

AKC Registration and Information
5580 Centerview Drive, Suite 200
Raleigh, NC 27606-3390
(919) 233-9767

Basset Hound Club of America
Mimi McCabe, Secretary
6414 E. Corrine Drive
Scottsdale, AZ 85264

Canadian Kennel Club
89 Skyway Avenue
Etobicoke, Ontario
Canada M9W 6R4

American Boarding Kennel Association
4575 Galley Road, Suite 440A
Colorado Springs, CO 80915

Orthopedic Foundation for Animals
2300 Nifong Blvd.
Columbia, MO 65201
(573) 442-0418

Magazines
Dog World
29 Wacker Drive
Chicago, IL 60606-3298
(312) 726-2802

Dog Fancy
P.O. Box 53264
Boulder, CO 80322-3264
(303) 666-8504

The Bugler
P.O. Box 698
McMinnville, TN 37110

Tally-Ho
(Through the Basset Hound Club
of America only)

Books
Alderton, David. *The Dog Care Manual*. Hauppauge, New York: Barron's Educational Series, Inc., 1986.
Baer, Ted. *Communicating With Your Dog*. Hauppauge, New York: Barron's Educational Series, Inc., 1989.
Walton, Margaret S. *The New Basset Hound*. New York, New York: Howell Book House, 1993.

Index